EVEREST
THE OLD WAY

These are my riches, these and the bright remembering
Of ridge and buttress and sky-shouldering spires;
These I shall count, when I am old, of an evening,
Sitting by the fire.

These words and the photograph of Mount Everest above, taken by
John Driskell in 1968, illuminate this book as 'A Bright Remembering'.
The verse is from a poem in *Showell Styles 'Mountaineers Week End Book'*,
published in 1952 and reprinted 1960. The author is unknown.

EVEREST
THE OLD WAY

An account compiled by
David Peckett, John Driskell,
and Les Simms,
using their diaries, letters, photographs and memories.

With thanks to Johnny Rudd, who generously gave
free access to his diaries and photographs.

bannister ● publications

Pre-publication Reviews

'From Barnsley to an empty Everest Base Camp in 1968 was a leap from the innocence of a dream into the richness of raw experience that this fascinating book brings so vividly to life. More than an important document of adventurous travel, the diary and letter narratives of these ordinary young travellers are always infused with the wonder and humility of those actually living out their Barnsley-based wanderlust.

'Today's trekkers will remark upon the differences and the recognitions in this book, but this is not the story of an exotic holiday. The return trip in 2010 adds a dimension of appreciation of the impact that all the absorbing observations and challenges of the 1968 experience had on the rest of their lives. Indeed, the production of this book is an act of celebration of a spirit that transforms an apparently 'modest' achievement into a landmark experience directing a lifetime ahead.'

Professor Terry Gifford
Centre for Writing and Environment, Bath Spa University,
Founding Director of the International Festival of
Mountaineering Literature 1987- 2008,
and Trustee of the Mountain Heritage Trust.

'I've done over 100 book reviews and I have to say that I enjoyed this book immensely. The journals were not written at the time with a view to a wider readership but they convey the experience and the whole context of Nepal, the Sherpas, and trekking with vivid immediacy. Their major strength is that they bring out individual perspectives, so that although describing the same things, there is no ... feeling of repetition.

'What you did was unusual, and it demanded planning, effort and determination. The point where you get to Base Camp and Kala Pattar is particularly moving.'

Kevin Boreman, formerly News Editor for High Magazine

First published in Great Britain in 2011 by

Bannister Publications Ltd
118 Saltergate
Chesterfield
Derbyshire S40 1NG

Copyright © John Driskell, David Peckett, Les Simms

ISBN 978-0-9566196-6-2

John Driskell, David Peckett, Les Simms assert their moral right
to be identified as the authors of this work

A catalogue record for this book is available from the British Library.

Typeset in Palatino Linotype and designed by
Escritor Design, Chesterfield, Derbyshire

Printed and bound in the UK by the
MPG Books Group, Bodmin and King's Lynn

Contents

Foreword	By Sir Christopher Bonington, CVO, CBE, DL	vii
Introduction	Acknowledgements	xi
Chapter 1	The Memories Beckon	1
Chapter 2	The Road to Kathmandu	9
Chapter 3	In Mystical Kathmandu	21
Chapter 4	Across the Foothills to the Khimti Kola	37
Chapter 5	Over Three Great Ridges into the Namche Valley	61
Chapter 6	Up the Dudh Kosi to Namche Bazaar	73
Chapter 7	To the Foot of the Mighty Everest	89
Chapter 8	Home Kaman and Don't Spare the Sherpa	119
Chapter 9	Return to India and Home	139
Postscript	"Live life to the full, blend dream with the deed"	165
Letters Home	Letters before and after the trek	166
Before and After	Photographs taken in 1968 and 2010	182
Biographies		190
Glossary		193

FOREWORD BY SIR CHRIS BONINGTON
CVO, CBE, DL

This is the story of a trek to Mount Everest at a time when few Westerners who were not part of a large national expedition had made the journey. It took place in 1968 during a five year period when expeditions to Mount Everest were not permitted: only five groups had successfully scaled the mountain at that time and as few as two dozen climbers had reached the summit.

The story is told through the diaries of young men who are now in their late sixties. They give a vivid picture of life in Nepal at a time when the country was waking up to the commercial possibilities of trekking. These were the forerunners of the extensive trekking industry of today and their experiences will fascinate readers.

In his book *Annapurna* the French climber Maurice Herzog describes the first ascent of an 8,000m peak and the epic struggle for survival on the descent. The very last line of that book reads 'There are other Annapurnas in the lives of men', recognising the challenges that people face in all walks of life. David Peckett, one of the authors of this book, faced his Annapurna at the age of 11 when he was admitted to Pinderfield's Hospital in Wakefield for a period of three years, much of the time encased in a plaster cast from his chest to his knees. By a remarkably poignant coincidence, the date of that admission to hospital was 29th May 1953, the very day that Edmund Hillary and Tensing Norgay became the first humans to stand on the summit of Mount Everest.

When planning an expedition there are two essential requisites: a clear goal to achieve, and a group of people who are motivated by the goal, dedicated to achieving it and ready to work as a team. This is the story of a group of young people who identified their goal, saved hard and planned for two years, resigned their jobs and set off to follow their ambitions.

I had first visited Nepal in 1960 as a member of the Nepalese, Indian, British Combined Services Expedition to Annapurna II, an unclimbed peak of 7937 metres and the following year joined a small expedition to Nuptse, the third peak of Everest. We started our approach march from Kathmandu as there were no roads or airstrips on the way to Everest and as a result none of the infrastructure of present day tourism. It wasn't very different in 1970 when I next visited Nepal on our expedition to the South Face of Annapurna. Commercial trekking was still in its infancy and Nepal still had a pristine quality. This is what John Driskell and his friends experienced. They were filled with excitement, wonder and all the joys of exploration on their journey to Nepal and on the 150 mile trek to the base of Mount Everest with the minimum of support. It is the kind of journey that can't be made today.

Mount Everest has attracted people for centuries. The Tibetan name 'Chomolungma' – Mother Goddess of the World – suggests that they knew it was the highest mountain long before it was officially declared the highest in the world and named after Sir George Everest in 1854. Climbers intent on reaching the summit were the first to be drawn, but when Nepal opened up, other people took the opportunity to travel. It drew the authors of this book to make the journey, all on a 'shoestring'; it seems incredible that the whole trek of 27 days cost a mere £33.00.

This book, with its diaries, letters and photographs, recently rescued and digitalised from rapidly deteriorating slides, and the memories revived by a return visit in 2010, is a unique record of its time.

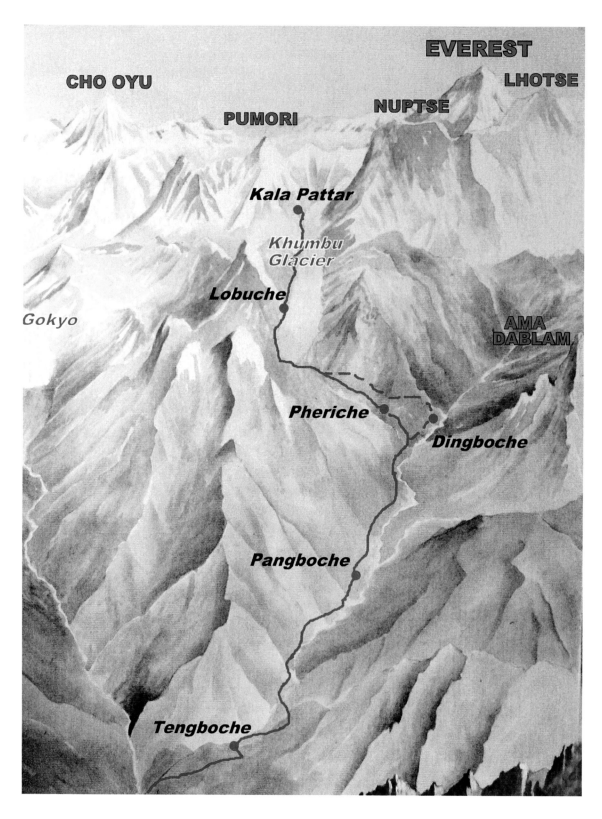

Acknowledgements

This book is more than simply the assembly of diaries, pictures and recollections. It represents the culmination of our early dreams and our expedition. The story of how it all began and how we relived the experience some 42 years later is described in the first chapter. We each had our own reasons for making this journey and for what we might achieve during the course of it. Now, looking back, we relive the wonder and magic of it all. The experience has enriched our lives and we hope that other, younger souls may be inspired to follow their own dreams to discover the wonder of the world and the people who make it so.

The production of this book owes much to many. Our particular thanks go to Jane Simms for all her work in editing our diaries; to Tom Blyth of Bannister Publications for his support, guidance and expertise; to Kevin Borman who read the original text and gave us encouragement; to Peter Race, Stacie Janney, Matt Padley and Race Cottam Associates, Sheffield, for producing the maps, and to Andy Birkby who painted views of our route. We also thank Owen and Julie Driskell for the 2010 photos and the many others who gave encouragement and helped us in smaller ways, including Kate Race, Pam Rudd, Andrew Simms, Liz Birkby, Louise Wilson, Robert Driskell and William Driskell.

Back in 1967, our friend Angus Stokes spent hours ensuring our Land Rover was fit for the journey. We owe a great deal to him. Our thanks also go to Mrs Robinson and Mrs Smith, close friends of David's mother, who helped in many ways, particularly with the sewing machine and in somehow acquiring thousands of different sized plastic bags. Mr and Mrs Joe Peckett, David's parents, readily shared their home on the farm as our expedition base.

Finally, our thanks go to Jill Driskell, Pam Peckett and Christine Simms for their forbearance, encouragement and support.

Facing Page: A painting by Andy Birkby of the final stage of the trek from Tengboche to Base Camp at Kala Pattar, described Chapter 7.

We become intoxicated by the sheer joy of remembering, in the very same places.

Chapter 1

The Memories Beckon

Email – johnldriskell to david.peckett

Dave, what about this? Two facts have come to my attention in the past few days. One, they now have luxury trekking lodges in the Himalaya. And two, Audley Travel has a Nepal specialist! Also, there's a road to Jiri – has been for several years. I've worked out it must cross the path we trekked, probably several times, and go through some of the villages we stayed in. What do you think? I'm getting a little excited! John

Email – david.peckett to johnldriskell

You have ruined my life – if you're suggesting what I think you are! I'm an old man thinking my travelling days are gone and then you come up with something irresistible. What a dream to go back. My mind is full of images, smells and memories. I've even got indigestion from the thought of mustard oil! I can just smell the wood smoke, hear the dogs and the early morning cockerels. To trek into the mountains and see some of the views and places we went to – wow! To find ourselves in Kathmandu, mystical Kathmandu, looking for the Camp Hotel – I can't sleep! David

It was enough. The idea was implanted. The memories stirred and we re-read our diaries.

1

Crowds gathered to look …

The plane from Delhi banks over the valley and there they are, the high Himalaya, huge, majestic, disdainful and unchanged. Kathmandu has certainly changed. The small medieval city we knew is now a vast sprawling metropolis with new houses springing up by the hour. Mobile phones only just outnumber the motorbikes. Our Kathmandu hotel has a roof terrace, a lift and a restaurant but, reassuringly, still no secure supply of electricity.

We reach Jiri in a very comfortable minibus and visit villages we once took four days to walk to and then slept in. We retrace our steps and stand with our photographs to determine the exact places. Crowds gather to look over our shoulders and wonder that 42 years ago these old men stood on the same spot. Very few of them were even born then.

All the villages have changed too. But our memories of the detail of those far-off days spring to life as we find the water source where we used to wash, the tree whose enormous trunk we rested against as we drank tea and dried our sweat-sodden clothes. We gaze into the depths of a deep valley and debate whether the suspension bridge spanning the glacier-charged river is the same one we walked over 42 years earlier.

Looking across the valleys and foothills we can trace the ridges and routes we followed. We admire the steep foothills that tier away towards the mighty snow-capped peaks. We climbed them once, trekked over them. We can remember almost every step. It is a joy that stiff and aching knees can't diminish. We become intoxicated by the sheer joy of remembering, in the very same places and with some of the very same people.

You would expect Nepal to have changed in almost half a century. New roads have been cut into hillsides, pylons carry power up terraced mountains and over ridges, plastic pipes snake water from streams to houses and villages, and the fact that everyone has a mobile phone makes the country feel even smaller, yet at the same time more connected to the rest of the world.

We are old men approaching 70, who have come to recall our youthful ambitions and relive some of the moments seared most vividly onto the retinas of our minds' eyes. With our memories revitalised we return home to search through diaries, letters, photographs, maps, sketches and the deep recesses of our minds for as much detail as possible of a trek that was truly worth remembering. We are engulfed by an incontinent avalanche of recollections.

How it started the first time

Once we were young and yearning for adventure. The Sixties were full of optimism and we were among the first to realise the opportunities in front of us. Bob Dylan's lyrics, *The times they are a-changing* and *But for the sky there are no fences facing* encapsulated the spirit of our age. And the world was inviting.

We were four men and one woman who met at teacher training college and planned the expedition for two years. The plan was conceived and promoted by John, whose energy and enthusiasm drew us together from a wider group of friends interested in mountaineering. He suggested that if we saved £10 a month (a quarter of our income) and perhaps worked during some of the holidays, within two years we could have amassed £300 each, enough to buy a long-wheel-base Land Rover and cover all the petrol and food expenses of a year's travel.

Five of us were sufficiently single-minded to see this plan through and on 6th November 1967 we left our base in Barnsley bound

for Nepal. We had planned a great deal but we had no set route or timetable, nor had we recourse to much in the way of local maps or guide books. There were many places we wanted to see, but we were entirely flexible and changed our plans almost daily when we met other travellers and heard their experiences. On our outward journey we travelled through Europe, Turkey, Iran, Pakistan and India to Nepal. However, our eventual trek to Mount Everest from Kathmandu was the highlight.

The only 'fence' was our budget, and we planned to travel for as long as the money lasted. We were entirely self-financing, and having taught for three years, were among the first to take what is now called 'a gap year'. The journey was ours; we were free to visit whatever and to wander wherever we wanted. Every day was an adventure, a voyage of discovery.

The overland route to India became known as the 'Hippy Trail', populated as it was by those set on 'finding' both themselves and the cheap cannabis available in India, Pakistan and Afghanistan. We were far from being hippies and our motivations and ambitions were very different. The journey overland had its difficulties and dangers but we rarely felt afraid. The world was opening up; roads were being built and travel becoming easier and that filled us with optimism. We loved it and we felt the world would always be as open, peaceful, accessible and as friendly as we found it.

Our diaries, written every day, tell the stories that still thrill us when we read them 42 years later. We remember Persepolis when we were the only tourists there and we camped right by the main gates. We spent Christmas camping out completely alone beneath the incredible night skies of the Iranian desert. In Fatehpur Sikri we camped right in the

'We spent Christmas camping out completely alone in the Iranian desert.'

heart of the complex of palaces and wandered in and out freely. We spent a day at the Taj Mahal with just a few Indian tourists and no other Europeans. And so on, until we arrived in Kathmandu.

Kathmandu in February 1968 was almost devoid of both vehicles and tourists, and most people went barefoot. There was only one company organising trekking, and no company organising trekking compatible with our budget! We stayed in a medieval house that catered for travellers and called itself 'Camp Hotel'. We lived and cooked in the one room we rented.

From there we hired a Sherpa, 'LP', to be our guide and he hired a porter, Kaman, to carry a hundredweight of food and equipment. Each of us carried about 30 pounds of personal gear. With LP and Kaman we spent 27 days in the 'Middle Ages' with no hotels, no lodging houses, no roads, not even a wheel. In the lower foothills we slept out on the thatched verandas of Nepalese houses. Once we reached Sherpa territory we slept in their houses, sharing the fireside with the family; we were taken into village houses and paid only for the firewood that we used for cooking.

The houses had no toilets, no running water, no electricity; they didn't even have candles or glass in the windows. But what they did have was warm hospitality and a complete acceptance of us as travellers in the mountains. Oh, and they also had rats and fleas! In some houses the animals lived on the ground floor and the family on the first floor above them. There was a wood fire set on a stone hearth in the middle of the floor for heating and cooking, but no chimney to carry the smoke away.

Today most trekkers fly in to the airstrip at Lukla, a village we reached after 11 days of walking. There were other trekkers, but so few that each one we met is mentioned in the diaries. At Gorak Shep, the original base camp for Mount Everest, we were completely on our own; there were no buildings, tents or litter, in fact not a sign of other humanity. There had been no expeditions to Everest since 1965 and it remained closed to climbers until 1969. This was due to hostile, near-warlike relations between India and China at the time, and the Nepalese didn't want anyone to provoke the Chinese.

The following account is the story, told through our diaries which we each kept and wrote daily. They are, of course, the same story seen through different eyes and some events are therefore recorded in both accounts. It is remarkable how different each account is, with David looking at the people and what they were doing and John much more interested in the sweep of the landscape. We have included both accounts almost exactly as they were written by somewhat unsophisticated young people, at times in rather arduous or stressful situations. They were never written with the intention of publication but were for the personal record of two people enthralled by the diaries of Captain Scott and other Polar explorers. It was a thrill to have them typed when the handwritten accounts began to fade and an even greater thrill to put them together in later years, when computers made it easy to do. We have added our memories, extracts from letters and also entries from the diary of Johnny Rudd who kept his account of the journey in a less systematic way than we did. We all had cameras and just as our 35mm slides were beginning to deteriorate, we have been able to resurrect them with the help of modern technology.

A Note from Les

I can't remember now how I first got involved in the overland expedition, since I wasn't interested in mountains and physical exercise was anathema to me. In spite of this and my initial misgivings I got swept along by the enthusiasm of the others. I'm glad I went. I loved the travel through countries, deserts and mountains, but the thought of trekking horrified me! The expedition turned out to be one of the most important experiences of my life, which I have been boring people with ever since. It introduced me to the most beautiful place I have ever been to, the foothills of the Himalaya.

We were a mixture of different personalities but by and large, the whole trip worked extremely well, due in large part to the combination of John's wild and constant enthusiasm and David's sensible and steadying influence.

Ironically, the highlight of the whole overland journey for me was, in retrospect, the trek to Namche Bazaar, even though after the first two days of slogging uphill I began to look for a village where I might stay until the other four returned. I didn't trek the last exhausting miles from Namche to Everest, but stayed in the village for five days.

I didn't keep a diary (well, only as far as Munich!) and my memory for detail isn't as sharp as David's or John's. In fact, I confess that I don't remember much of what follows in their accounts. But what will stay with me for ever is the atmosphere of the place, the sights and smells, the sense of being cut off from civilisation and the knowledge that the only way back was to walk. The smell of wood smoke still powerfully evokes memories of LP and Kaman cooking up huge quantities of rice over an open fire in some idyllic location at the end of an exhausting day. Surprisingly, despite the exhaustion and my grumbles at the start, by the end of the trek I was fitter than I have ever been – either before or since – and the ease with which I was romping over the hills was a source of immense exhilaration and satisfaction.

I am very grateful to John and David for reminding me of all this by means of their diaries, and hope that this collection of words and pictures will keep those memories alive and be of continual interest – to us if no-one else.

Chapter 2

The Road to Kathmandu

We begin with the diary entries for the 11th February 1968 as we leave Muzaffarpur in India and head for the Nepalese border. Our destination was Kathmandu. To reach it we had to cross a huge ridge 2582m high, before descending into the Kathmandu Valley. This road, called the Raj Path, was built in the early 1950s by the Indian Government and is a tortuous route now supplanted by a longer one which follows the river valley. Before that, there was no road to Kathmandu. We hoped to find a campsite or a cheap place to stay and from there find out how possible it was to trek to Mount Everest. It was just over three months since we had left Barnsley in Yorkshire.

Sunday 11ᵗʰ February

Lush banana groves, bamboos and palm trees grow in profusion   *David …*
amid the rice and wheat fields. Most palm trees are mutilated by the efforts to collect oil. The efforts seem reasonable, but surely people must know that stripping off all the bark kills the tree. Fodder gatherers seem to lack that knowledge too; almost every tree has been stripped so many times that they grow in the most horrible shapes. Worst of all are the woodcutters, who just chop off the bark around some old branch, helping to kill the tree. Strangely though, all the dead trees don't seem to get chopped up. We saw a man shin nimbly up a palm tree to position a flask to gather the oil. He linked his arms around the trunk and used a band slipped over his ankles to give purchase.

Most of the roadside is a continuous village: huts of rush or mud

A faint line appeared on the horizon, grew stronger, and another became discernible further away. At last we were in sight of the Himalaya!

surrounded by small rush shelters for stores or animals; beautiful dove-cotes perched on high poles. The dovecotes are built on a wheel, set high on a pole and thatched. Fuel cakes changed from dry chapatti-type to ingot shaped, stacked to dry.

Though we stared hard into the north we could see no hills at all. Several herds of cattle stand around in their overcoats of sacking; I can't work out whether they are for warmth or to keep the sun off. Nearly all the bullock-cart drivers ride along asleep on the load. The animals just plod along slowly; they don't stick to the left and at the blare of a horn nothing happens. Only after blasting to wake the driver does the cart slowly veer off to the side.

We crossed one rather wobbly bridge. To safeguard the narrow bridges, speed breakers are built into them: two ridges six or so inches high which would give the vehicle a real bang. All warning signs are in Hindi so our drivers have to be alert for these dangers.

Nearer the border a bus rolled past with a capacity load. People overflowed from the inside, covering the whole roof and back. I should think well over a hundred people travelled on that single-decker thirty-seater coach. At Raxaul it was unloading and the entire street seemed full of disembarking passengers. Women in this northern area have rings through their noses, encrusted with stones or engraved and covering the top lip and mouth.

Raxaul was another nightmare, solidly blocked with the usual traffic, bullock carts in particular. Some are bamboo framed and covered in cloth like the covered wagons of the Hollywood 'Westerns'. They look very comfortable for the sleeping driver!

In the bazaar we struggled to find the vegetable section. No one could direct us to it; then we found a whole street full of just vegetables. Each portion of the market is usually allotted to one trade or set of goods, and once you're familiar with the layout you can buy anything. We saw one man haggling for bananas. After seeing his price we went to buy some. The fellow then joined in on the side of the salesman, trying to sell them at double what he had paid. We saw ploughs for sale, each component roughly hewn to shape, just needing to be bolted together. The wooden plough share had no metal tip.

The Customs and Police check posts were the least efficient yet. All the usual bureaucracy we encountered when entering India – carnets, currency declaration forms and so on – was lost here. This man asked questions but didn't seem bothered by our negative replies. He had to write all the normal forms, but did so twice. At the police post no one came, so I went back to the Customs man to ask him what to do. He told me to fill in one of the forms then we could leave! However, the policeman came back in time to stamp our passports.

To enter Nepal the road crossed a very narrow bridge jammed with tongas and carts. There were still no hills in sight. A man with a mongoose and snakes tried to entertain us as we sat patiently waiting.

The first town in Nepal is Birganj. It is a kind of a mixture of Indian and Nepalese. The dwellings slowly thinned until we crept into open Nepal. Peasant houses set on stilts peeped out of the dense forest. Low forested hills came into view, cut by a deep gorge. The road followed the gorge, crossing it in several places. During the thaws and rains the mighty torrents will fill the whole bed.

Staying at a forest rest house, where the air smells gorgeous and the trees seem cleaner. Again the culture has changed since we crossed the invisible border line. Strong little men with Mongol features, carrying huge loads by a band passed across the forehead – all as we expected to find, but perhaps not quite so immediately. A small boy came to visit. His eyes filled with wonder, he sighed with ecstasy at our treasures.

☙

John ...   The good road ended soon after Muzaffarpur and we were back on the usual single carriageway. We travelled along in a mood of eager anticipation and I kept my eyes fixed on the hazy horizon. At Motihari, still with no view of the mountains, we filled up with petrol and oil in readiness for the vehicle's 9,000 mile service. We pressed on 20 miles to Raxaul, the India border town, but still no sight of the hills. As we entered the town we stopped at a Tourist Office to get some information. Practically everything they told us we later found to be wrong, including the date!

Dave and I went shopping and wandered for ages through the market before finding the vegetable street, but eventually we got all our requirements and returned to the Land Rover.

The Customs post was hardly noticeable and we had to ask to find it. The Customs officer, though inefficient as usual, was very friendly and I had a chat with him about British history, of all things. We then moved on to the Nepal Customs post which proved to be equally unobtrusive. This was the least formal border crossing we had encountered.

Once inside Nepal we noticed the more Mongoloid features of the inhabitants, many of whom were wearing the traditional Nepalese hats. The road was straight and we drove along at a good speed but there were still no mountains. In fact it was completely flat. Then a faint line appeared on the horizon and grew stronger, and another line became discernible further away. At last we were in sight of the Himalaya! I had this feeling of excitement and joy and pressed hard on the accelerator to bring them closer. They formed a beautiful line and seemed to represent a faint and mystic challenge, a distant symbol of adventure and romance, and the embodiment of early British mountaineer Frank Smythe's 'distant view'.

The ground began to rise gently and cut a straight line through forests of tall deciduous trees. Then the road started to wind more steeply uphill and we caught glimpses through the trees of steep wooded hillsides with slight traces of billowy cloud clinging to them. At the side of the road were sharp pinnacles of moraine, a result of seasonal torrents. On the other side of the road was the wider river bed, with no water but covered with round pebbles of all sizes – another reminder of the vicious post-monsoon floods. Round and up, over and around bumps, passing Sherpas with stout thighs (a great change from India), carrying loads on their headbands.

We reached a town and asked for a tourist bungalow. A very helpful, smiling Sherpa not only told us of one but showed us the way in his Red Cross Volkswagen and sent word to the chowkidar (or caretaker). As we waited outside in beautiful surroundings with views of the mountains and that fine mountain smell in the air, a smiling little Sherpa boy arrived and showed great interest in us. He left after a while, not becoming a pest as many would have done.

The Nepalese, squat and stocky with Mongoloid eyes and ready smiles, seem happy and friendly. You feel great respect for them. Nepal is, after all, home of the famous Gurkha soldiers and Sherpa porters.

The bungalow was very comfortable and that evening we sat on the moonlit veranda in armchairs chatting to a fellow from the Indian High Commission to Kathmandu. It looked like being an interesting run the next day. What a joy it is to be in hills again after the flat, crowded plains of India.

❧

Johnny …

With 9050 miles on the clock, the journey from Muzaffarpur to Raxaul was fairly uneventful as Indian journeys go. We travelled through the usual busy villages and fairly fertile agricultural areas, where water had been controlled and used effectively. However, areas without proper irrigation were drought-ridden and eroded wastelands. Palms grow in abundance, growing alternatively thinner and fatter from bottom to top where they have been mutilated to gather oil. The other trees that seemed to thrive were mangroves – huge things with extra trunks growing from suckers that trail from the branches to take root. Bananas with their curious flowers were as common as beech trees in England.

❧

Monday 12th February

David …

What a day. To begin at the beginning, dawn over the Himalaya filled the valley with golden mist. Thatched huts looked comfortably warm against the cold fresh air. Once we were on the road the village, busy with porters, soon fell behind. About four miles along, the road came to a halt and turned into the river bed. Jogging along, we were suddenly confronted by the river rushing before us in a typical, clear, mountain torrent. Obviously, others had gone through and so must we. The water must have been two feet deep in the centre. Negotiating it was exciting, though not a problem. Further up we had to cross the river several times.

One crossing almost brought us to our knees. Mid-stream we stopped and having not engaged four-wheel drive, the water pressure was too much for the Land Rover and the engine stalled. Panicking, we jumped out, fully clothed into the water. Pushing was useless, especially as Les had the brakes on as he tried to start the engine. By a stroke of good fortune the exhaust pipe was just clear of the torrent. As I looked, feeling blank, up she started and John plunged in to the water with the wheel brace to turn on the four-wheel drive. Out she went, dripping but safe. Our panic turned to delighted laughter as we emerged from the river, boots full, trousers soaked, but happy.

On and on, up and up, for ever upwards went the road, snaking, winding, curling upwards. The scenery began with low, densely forested hills; behind them were more foothills, some dense with timber, others neatly terraced. I would remark, "How big? Crikey, look at that!" Then we would find ourselves up above the hill we had recently been exclaiming at.

Out she went, dripping but safe.

14

Below, the hillsides were carefully, immaculately stepped. Wherever the hill was not vertical, men have cultivated. Browns and reds, shot with new green, or freshly dug. Far over to the left a peak loomed over the forest. Drops below the road were unbelievable and landslides, a common danger, blocked or damaged the road in several places. Hardy Nepalese men, small and sinewy, were shovelling soil down the hillside to clear the road. Peasants steadily paced up or down, their mighty packs held by the famous headbands. Children carried their packs in similar fashion; they must be taught from birth for them to be able to use their muscles like that.

After topping several ridges, each one allowing us to see just a little more of the hills, John was bubbling with excitement. Then behold, there they were, not too clear, but so bright, the eternal snows! We stared silently, our eyes scanning from side to side.

At Daman we rushed up the viewing tower, trying to work out what was where. "There's Annapurna; that's Gauri Sankar; that must be Everest. No! That's definitely Makalu. Where's Kanchenjunga?" And so on as we sat, awe inspired, to eat our meal of tomatoes, bananas and bread.

Still, Kathmandu seemed a long way over the next set of hills, especially as we discovered a broken rear spring. It must have happened in one of the fords. Our spare will be used after all.

Valley after valley, contoured with terraces, populated with reed dwellings or thatched timber huts. Brown, smiling faces of the Nepalese people greeted us in the villages. Again we noted the amazing change when we arrive in a new country – a complete change of race, no similarity at all in size or shape. Banana trees and bamboo grow everywhere among the rich woods. Peasant farmers pace along with enormous packs of firewood slung from their headbands.

About four o'clock we reached Kathmandu Valley. It is far bigger than I anticipated; a wide, flat valley, hidden from the world for centuries. Buildings spread along the centre, faintly obscured by the evening mist. Kathmandu, the mystical name that has thrilled travellers from all parts. Thick, billowing cloud completely hid the mountains. After our usual struggle to get to know the town we established ourselves in the Hotel Opera, quite cheap, but not really to our liking.

John ...   We set off early with high expectations of soon being in Kathmandu. The road wound along the wooded hillside by the bed of the river until we came to a barrier that signposted a diversion. A track led to the river bed and we came to a ford. It was deeper than we had expected but we got through.

However, we came to another and then another which looked terribly deep. We plunged through but halfway across the unthinkable happened – the engine stalled. A look of panic crossed Les's face as he tried to restart it, and we all leapt out into the knee-deep water and waded round to the back. Fortunately the exhaust pipe was an inch above the water. The starter motor rattled and eventually, to the relief of us all, the engine spluttered back to life. Spurts of water poured out of the exhaust and all was well with the engine. However, if it was to have enough power to break the resistance of the water, it had to be in 4-wheel drive. I took the wheel brace and groped for the relevant nut, with the full force of the mountain torrent bursting over it. When that was done the Land Rover pulled easily on to the bank. A nasty few moments, but all was well, with nothing worse than four sopping wet pairs of trousers.

There were more fords but none as bad as that one and we were soon on the road again. The next section of the road was quite incredible. It rose in bend after bend, winding back on itself with the most alarming drops over the side. You could look up and see the road climbing above you in the most ridiculous places.

After the river crossings it took four hours of continuous ascent to reach the top of the hill, and just before we did so we caught our first glimpse of the eternal snows in the form of an immense snow peak appearing through the trees. At the top we beheld a fantastic view of a vast array of peaks and snowfields.

We hurried down the 200 feet or so to the viewing tower in Daman and rushed to its top, armed with binoculars. 'Vast' and 'beautiful' are thoroughly inadequate words to describe the sight which met us. We could see from Kanchenjunga to Annapurna, including Everest, Gauri Sankar and Dhaulagiri. Through the binoculars the peaks looked even more beautiful and you could fully appreciate the magnificence of their distant bulk. Fluted walls of ice that must have been thousands of feet high led up to delicately pointed snow summits. We absorbed the view as we ate our lunch.

Afterwards, during the long twisting descent through the terraced hills, I almost dropped asleep now the air of excitement had gone. As we descended, the terraces were cultivated with wheat and rice. I suppose cultivation gradually moved upwards as the year progressed. When we reached the bottom we realised we faced yet another climb before reaching Kathmandu.

We beheld a fantastic view of a vast array of peaks and snowfields.

At the dinner stop, Les noticed that the main leaf of a rear spring had cracked – it must have happened in the ford. As we topped the pass to Kathmandu, the land spread out before us in an unexpectedly flat way, and we could see the city sprawled on the broad valley floor. After two police checks we were in Kathmandu, looking for somewhere to camp or stay. We followed a taxi that showed us the way to the Hotel Opera where, after a bit of haggling, we decided to stay. Twenty rupees per night and we weren't allowed to cook in the room, so we ate in their cheap restaurant with a group of Canadians from Vancouver.

We took a short fast walk before going to bed. The city was strangely medieval. The streets were wider than those in Varanasi, but the buildings were only three storeys high, with a lot of woodwork – much like the Shambles in York.

☙

An immense snow peak appeared through the trees.

Johnny ...

After our adventure in the fords we were back on the main road with no bigger problem than four pairs of wet shoes and trousers. These would dry today; the engine would have taken considerably longer.

The road, the Raj Path, was getting steeper and higher all the time. Steeply wooded hills soared up to the blue sky and below us terraced fields and forest, containing the most exquisite trees, fell like a green waterfall to the ribbon of silver that was the river below. Up and up, on and on, for everlasting miles the road hugged its way up the hills. We asked ourselves how much longer could we climb, how much tighter could the hairpins be?

At Daman we spent a long time gazing at this great panorama, each one of us thinking our own thoughts, each silent or bubbling as the mood took us. I can see full reason for the sacrifice that we, mere mortals, have made to stand on the proud heads of these vast mountains. Love, fear and many other emotions course through my veins at the sight of the Himalaya.

We drive on, descending as dizzily as we ascended, to the valley. Up another rise and there before us is the huge hidden valley of Kathmandu. Every inch of this valley is cultivated and in its centre lies the city of Kathmandu, its skyline formed by the spires of a million

The road twisted through terraced fields into the Kathmandu valley.

temples and palaces. We reach its centre with some difficulty, through narrow chaotic medieval streets overhung with timbered buildings.

After haggling for a price we take a room in the Hotel Opera. We have a meal for 12s 0d. We settle to sleep. There is much to be done tomorrow.

'LP', our Sherpa

*Kaman, hired by LP from the streets
of Kathmandu*

Chapter 3

In Mystical Kathmandu

Tuesday 13th February

Breakfast on the hotel lawn in the hot sun is so pleasant after the much colder nights here.

David …

From there we walked along the wide streets to the British Embassy, where John enquired about visiting the Prince and Princess of Nepal. At the Tourist Office we had little joy; the man's curt answers were unhelpful. We wanted a camp site or a cheap hotel where we could cook in the room (imagine wanting that in England). The Camp Hotel seemed the most likely but was 20 rupees (13s 6d) per day. A money changer in the street told us of a hotel which might let us camp in the grounds. They refused, but told us of another, which turned out to be the one we stayed in last night. It appears that because of 'beatniks' in the past, camping is now forbidden. By late afternoon we had returned to Camp Hotel and were established in two quaint rooms.

In the old narrow city streets, temples mix with the shops and old palaces of the Rana regime stand high above the three-storey dwellings. Houses rich with carving hang over the streets. It's like a historical view of the Middle Ages in London but it is common, daily life here. Religious idols sit in every corner, where worshippers stop to pay their respects. Erotic figures, carved or painted, cover temples or archways over the road.

Tibetan refugees, beautiful wrinkled people, trudge along looking quite lost. Their priests, the Lamas, wear thick orange robes and thick felt boots. Others wear a thick blanket round their middle that serves as both shawl and blanket. Two battalions of Gurkhas march past to the huge parade ground. These famous fighting men of the hills seem especially dignified on their own ground. Legends run behind them, reflected from the curved knives on their hips. Small Tibetan children try to sell me a 'genuine' prayer wheel that contains writings by "the Dalai Lama himself".

The English spoken by the Nepalese is superior to that of the average Indian or Pakistani. Neither do they seem to have any of the strange Indian twists of language. Few people bother us, unlike in India.

All day the peaks gradually cleared until the twin peaks of the mighty Gauri Sankar filled the horizon. As we shopped at dusk many people thronged into the temples or worshipped at the wayside effigies, some lighting candles or splashing themselves with holy water.

୨

John … Had a slightly inadequate breakfast, and then set about our day's business. We first went to the British Embassy, a fine building set in nice grounds. I picked up a letter and we found out where to enquire about Sherpas. Our next call was at the Tourist Office, but the staff there were singularly unhelpful. Pam and I visited the Camp Hotel which had quite good rooms available at good prices, but the Land Rover would have to be left in the street.

In the meantime the others had been changing money at the rate of 13 rupees to the dollar. We then visited the Post Office, where we picked up bundles of mail, and continued on to the Royal Hotel to enquire about camping, but without any luck. They directed us back to a place which proved to be the hotel where we were already staying. They wouldn't allow us to camp either, so we had a quick meal and left to take up residence at the Camp Hotel, a bit Spartan but with a great deal of atmosphere.

A frustrating day really, but we saw a good bit of the city. It was cleaner and less crowded than the towns in India.

୨

Johnny … Our rooms at the Camp Hotel are clean and tidy. We climb a bending flight of stairs and the roof is too low to be able to stand

22

upright. The place must be 500 years old. The atmosphere is unbelievable. Our room is low and long. Gallery windows are opened and closed by wooden shutters. The ceiling is beamed and warped. It is beautiful here.

The most interesting people are the Tibetans, their coarse brown skin wrinkled by the harsh mountain winds, in long flowing cloaks, pigtails and wispy beards. They give the impression of tremendous strength and, at the same time, beautiful gentleness. They are shy and seem a little mesmerised by this new world where the motor car is only just catching on. They look lost and huddle together as they tread carefully through the alien streets in their great boots of red and black wool.

Wednesday 14th February

David ...

Another hectic day of arranging, so that I have not yet seen much of the city. I love the atmosphere, so like a village with its rural people and the clean, bright air. I began by scouring the shops for bread and chasing some mythical rickshaw boy who sells it. Eventually we

The view from the back of the Camp Hotel.

found some in a backstreet café. After a large breakfast of cornflakes, fried eggs, tomatoes and bread, Les and I took the Land Rover to the garage for repairs. It took about two hours for two men to do the job. The cost? Thirteen shillings and sixpence, without having to argue. No doubt we could have got down to ten shillings, but the browbeating is so frustrating. I always feel that I am being unreasonable in my demands, despite knowing I have been robbed.

Met an English couple and their young family having their Land Rover welded on the shock absorbers. They have had many accidents compared with us. We seem to have been extremely lucky so far: we've only killed a pig!

Johnny and John went to try to organise the trek, and we were disappointed to find out it would be 'impossible' to get just one porter. But it turns out that the Camp Hotel (what an organisation this place is!) has its own Sherpa. He's out trekking at the moment but should be back later this week, when we can hire him. So the Everest trek looks like being on. To extend our visa and get a trekking permit we need two more photographs plus ten forms. Then the hotel got the 'Yeti Travel Bureau' to ring up the Prince, and we have an appointment tomorrow at four.

The Camp Hotel is a quaint old backstreet four-storey house with carvings decorating the timber front. Wooden grilles cover the windows. Inside, the dark narrow staircase is set between crude panelled walls. Our room is very low, with one wall of shuttered windows. There is no glass. The ceiling is narrow, comprising closely set beams with riven planks above them. The other wall is panelled and everything is whitewashed. The room has a cosy atmosphere, as has the whole building. At home we would call it dirty, probably a slum dwelling. Here I am loving it.

John and Pam are upstairs in the next building, overlooking the street. From their window we have watched the world below, including yet another procession, led by drummers and cymbal players, behind them a string of men carrying baskets of food on bamboo yokes. The men roll their weight from side to side in order to carry the enormous loads; the bamboo takes the spring.

Much later more drummers, swelled by pipers this time, led a long procession of men and women in separate groups. The crowds were composed of the more Mongol-looking people; perhaps this was a religious festival? They came up the street, went into a house at the top, out of the back door and down the next street. Women wore gay colours, bright ribbons and tassels in their hair, their blanket-shawls wrapped round their waists and flung over their shoulders. They all carried an ornate silver box or a container of food, with rice, nuts, yogurt or spices. Behind them the men were dressed in black waistcoats and Jodhpur trousers. Some of the men had flowers in their hair. Others carried a stick with something resembling a horse-brass on the end. Others carried burning joss sticks and each one carried a gift.

Other sights of the day included a small boy, full Sherpa face with rosy cheeks and his ragged shirt not covering his bare backside, playing in manure as though it was Plasticine. For a while he practised making fuel chapattis, then he turned to modelling. All the time he sang to himself in a high-pitched warbling voice. Tibetan men or women, I couldn't always decide, passed several times, their hair in tight plaits pulled around their heads. They wear a thick black overcoat-cum-cloak which wraps around them, black trousers and long woven boots, a thick leather strip stitched on for the sole, crimpled at the edges like a moccasin.

One small boy passed by from the local slaughter house carrying two legs of a cow; another came later with the severed head on his shoulders. Youths came in from the gardens heaving great baskets of vegetables on their yokes and smoking away. Women had babies slung on their backs.

Down the street in the 'Shambles' of Kathmandu, we watched women wash themselves by a water pump, lathering their hair and wetting their saris through so that the fabric clings to their legs. Animals live on the ground floor in many houses; the family survives above. Fifteen buffalo skulls lay rotting in the sun near a spring that was channelled to run along a carved stone trough. Buffalo hides are flung over the wall to cure in the sun. Water buffalo are tethered by their front feet to poles set in the ground, one foot to each pole, and dogs with horribly diseased skin roam everywhere.

Children play what look to us to be complicated games of marbles. In every country so far we have seen marbles being played. A Tibetan offered us hashish in the street. It looked like a huge twist of tobacco. It is legal here but we have never been tempted. Many people want to buy our Land Rover.

Some of the other Europeans here are mixed-up souls. 'Nepal Lawrence' in his white turban and chocolate-brown Punjabi suit. 'High-travel' in his Afghan jacket, calf-length boots and shaven head. Others imitate the blanket-shawl look; some have beads and rings.

There are few vehicles in Kathmandu, no bullock carts or trolleys; all goods are moved by humans, carried on their backs or on yokes.

✌

John ...   David and Les were given the task of getting the Land Rover repaired. Johnny and I were to find out about trekking, while Pam stayed at the hotel to do odd jobs.

Our first call was at the 'Tiger Tops' office where the sought-after Miss Holly said she couldn't help us with any information about getting to Mount Everest. At the Yeti Travel Bureau they were very helpful , but unable to obtain porters for our planned trek. We were told that you can rarely get just one porter and that food en route through the foothills was scarce. We were advised to ask at the Camp Hotel. So we returned there and after a cup of tea asked the owner about porters and he said straight away that he could fix us up.

Shortly afterwards we met Les and David who had had the spring fixed for 20 rupees. Things were looking up!

At the surprisingly efficient Nepalese Secretariat we filled in forms and were assured there should be no trouble in extending our visa and getting a permit to go to Mount Everest. We needed two photographs, which we undertook to give them next day.

Back again to the Yeti Travel Bureau who rang up the residence of the Prince and Princess of Nepal and made an appointment for us. Success – we would be picked up at 4.00pm the next afternoon. (I had been given the 'calling card' of the Princess during a State visit to Britain the previous summer when she visited The Outward Bound School where I was working). Joyfully we returned to the hotel to tell the others the news.

We had a cup of tea and then went to have our photographs taken. They were promised for next day. As dusk fell Les and I went for a walk through the backstreets where the medieval atmosphere lent by the half-timbered, red- brick, thatched houses was made all the more authentic by the squalor. The silhouettes of Buddhist architecture and distant hills made for a beautiful skyline. We were all rather excited about the morrow.

Every convenience available at the Camp Hotel …

Thursday 15th February

Gargling pigeons busy all morning outside my window. The demolition 'workers' across the yard were busy too, banging away at a very early hour. Pity for the residents on the second floor of the house: their front wall of cotton sheets won't keep out much noise. I think they are just altering the front, which has been demolished. Everything else remains, even the clock ticking on the wall.

David …

Les and I revisited the Embassy to check up on protocol. We must call him 'Kumar', the Nepali word for Prince; the Princess is 'Your Royal Highness'. They could not help with garage accommodation. We visited the British Council Library to read some newspapers. The most recent was 3rd February but it was good to read of home and the various happenings.

Strange how we begin to accept all Europeans as kin; it makes me realise how much we have in common with them. We greet them all, French, German, Benelux, Australian, American, almost as fellow-countrymen.

It must have been market day; each square was busy with crowds

Posing for a photo with the Kumar outside the Royal Bungalow in the palace grounds. This was a rare outing for our best clothes!

milling around the various piles of sacks of nuts, rice, flour, beans, wool and so on. People who we earlier presumed to be Tibetans are in fact from near the border. But other Nepalese with ethnic connections to the Tibetans were about in great numbers, the men with their hair plaited with red ribbon and looped around their head. Women leave their plaits hanging down their backs; the young babies slung on their backs find them amusing toys.

Masses of soldiers in the parade ground; we discover they are rehearsing for Independence Day on the 18th. We should be here to see it.

After dinner we busied ourselves washing and smartening up. Out came the white shirts, the ties, shoes and cufflinks. With freshly-combed hair and beards we left for Yeti Travel. On the way a shoe-shine boy did an immaculate job, spending a full 15 minutes on my shoes. I have never had them so shiny.

Shortly after 4.00pm a fawn Volkswagen arrived to collect us. We squeezed in and were promptly delivered to the Princess' rather plain bungalow. It appears that the palace is being altered or rebuilt and that this is a temporary abode. Servants rushed around opening gates and car doors for us. At the door the Kumar greeted us. After being introduced, John presented the shield of the Outward Bound School to him. We sat and talked for a while until joined by the

Princess. Tea, cakes and peanut butter sandwiches were served. Les managed to throw his cake on the floor and Johnny almost spilled his tea, but otherwise all went well. We talked mainly of Britain and their official visit. He showed us the official photographic souvenir presented to them. The Princess said not a word the whole time, so we don't think she can speak English too well. A large Chow and a Tibetan terrier ran freely around, as servants padded silently by.

The Kumar was a very pleasant man indeed, openly answering our questions about Nepal, royal visits and so on. Before leaving, I told him of our problem of wanting to lock the Land Rover away. He very kindly offered to clear a garage at the palace for us. So when we go trekking 14 SRB goes to the palace!

Ⓘn the morning Johnny, Pam and I went to pick up our passport photos and then to the Secretariat to pick up our visa extensions and trekking permit. We had to wait there for an hour or so while the documents were made out. Meanwhile Les and Dave had been to the British Embassy to see if there was any mail and to enquire about formalities for this afternoon.

John …

We met back at the hotel at dinner time and spent the afternoon washing and getting shoes cleaned and I collected my trousers after having them pressed. At about half past three, arrayed in our smartest attire, we walked through the streets towards the Yeti Travel Agency where we were to be picked up.

After ten tense minutes a driver turned up in a Volkswagen and we were taken to the Royal residence. Another man rushed out to open the gate and yet another to open the car door as it pulled to a stop. We were shown into the bungalow by yet another helper. The outside seemed a little bare but the room we were ushered into was quite regal. The Kumar breezed in and shook us all by the hand, asking us to sit down in deep purple armchairs. After a short time we all relaxed and talked freely. The beautiful white Chow and Tibetan terrier were a contrast to the mangy skeletal dogs we had been seeing outside.

A servant brought tea and cakes, and we were joined by the Princess. We were shown the album of their visit to Britain, including photos of Ullswater Outward Bound School with Squadron Leader

Call in, said the prince

THE invitation teacher John Driskell received from the Prince of Nepal was a homely one.

"Call in and see the Princess and myself at the palace when you are in Nepal," said the prince when he visited the Outward Bound School at Ullswater, where John was teaching.

Yesterday John, aged 24, of Brigg Preparatory School, Brigg, Lincs, his fiancé, Pamela Archer, 25, of Feniscowles, Blackburn, and three other schoolteacher friends set off from Barnsley, Yorkshire, on a 20,000 mile overland round trip to India and Nepal.

There they will take the prince at his word.

The five saved hard for two years to finance the £1,800 trip. They expect to be away about nine months.

Daily Express Nov. 67.

Our invitation to meet the Prince captured the interest of the national press.

29

Lester Davies and Alan Roberts. It seemed strange, this far from home, to be shown a picture of my former boss and my fellow instructor and friend standing by a Land Rover outside the front of the School.

When the Princess and the Kumar made their visit and we were all formally introduced to them, it was Alan who told them I intended to visit Kathmandu and this led directly to our invitation. We broached our problem of where to leave the Land Rover and he immediately suggested that we could leave it in his garages. We said goodbye and were driven off in the Volkswagen.

A very enjoyable afternoon and quite a feather in our caps!

ꔷ

Johnny ... When we entered the room there was no formality whatsoever as the Kumar, in sweater and slacks, strode up to shake our hands. We made a presentation and were ushered into a huge set of armchairs. There was a short silence until we started talking and then there were no problems at all. We talked a lot about England and what he had seen there and about many topics of Nepalese culture and ways of life.

Friday 16ᵗʰ February

David ... John and I went to Patan, a town to the south of Kathmandu. On the way we called to post letters and John managed to get a stamp with a mountain on it for his letter. As we left, a yellow Land Rover from The Camp offered to give us a lift to Patan. We were sure we had met this Land Rover before at Persepolis. During conversation it turned out that these people had bought the Land Rover from the man and two women we had met there – small world.

Patan has changed little in a thousand years, I imagine. The progress that is gradually transforming Kathmandu has not yet touched the surrounding townships. Each street was an uneven cobbled surface; drains ran quite quickly along the side. As usual they were stinking, disease-carrying sewers. No attempt is been made to cover them. Decaying red brick and timber houses cling tightly to the darkened streets. Below, the tiniest rooms, dark and untidy, proved to be shops, one a butcher's with more offal than meat for sale, or at least on show. Temples filled every square, one with a large brass lion and a dragon flanking the doorway.

As the mountains were fairly clear, we walked north out of the town, dropping down the hill that Patan is built on. Women lazed in the sun, washing or feeding their many full-faced children. Their little smile and "Hello" or "Bye-bye" is marred by their ill-kempt appearance; poor kids with horrible running noses, dried skin on their cheeks, and dirty. Parents seem very similar to all parents in their love for their children, playing and making them smile.

Far to the north, clear of human influence, the mountains lazed in the noonday sun. Once out of the village among the beautifully kept terraced fields, we sat and stared, soaking in the sun and the peace, for a while.

Later, back in Kathmandu, Les and I walked by the river watching the locals do their washing. As the sun set behind the fiery clouds, sharp lances of light scanned across the valley, spot-lighting the various temples capped with gold or brass.

Once, Nepal was a series of small kingdoms and each valley town was a separate kingdom; I think there were 80. One particular kingdom, Gurkha, grew very strong among the perpetually warring states. Gradually it conquered all Nepal, unifying it for the first time. So mighty was the Gurkha army that it began conquering Indian territory. It was at that time that the British appeared on the scene and waged many campaigns against the Gurkhas. When peace was settled, the British Army incorporated some of the Gurkha regiments into the Indian Army because of their impressive fighting against the British. Ever since then there have been Gurkha regiments serving Britain, although the recent economies mean the number is being reduced. Also, although there is still a town called Gurkha, the title of the Gurkha Regiment is a misnomer, as the soldiers come from the whole of Nepal.

৵

After a leisurely breakfast, Dave and I set off on a bit of a sightseeing jaunt. We called in at the Post Office and just down the road were picked up by an English guy who had bought the yellow Land Rover we saw at Persepolis from its original owner. He took us

John ...

to Patan, where we wandered through the streets, which really did have a medieval atmosphere. There were no modern shops and the roads were hardly suitable even for jeeps. In the backstreets it smelt like a lavatory, with pigs grovelling in deep open sewers and a bone meal yard to the side. It was as bad as India, although there were no crowds. Women, stripped to the waist, were washing at the village water hole and others were washing in water that I'm sure wouldn't clean anything. We walked back through neatly cultivated fields and on to the riverside.

Spent a leisurely afternoon doing very little. We relaxed in our dimly-lit, low-roofed, comfortable little room and gazed across the street at brick walls and glassless windows. The street below was always full of vivid life and during the evening a full-scale, improvised jazz band played in the street.

Saturday 17ᵗʰ February

David … Today continued with a bang after a very leisurely beginning. I was just going round to have breakfast when the manager told me they had found a Sherpa who would be back in one hour. We had our usual excellent breakfast of cornflakes, fried bread, fried tomatoes, two fried eggs and tea. I could see quite a few Nepalese hanging about in the street so I went see if our Sherpa was there. Sure enough a little grinning man was picked out. He introduced himself, shook hands and beamed – all Sherpas beam in expedition photographs. I shouted to John to join me and then began our arrangements with haste.

The Sherpa's name turned out to be 'LP', very short initials for his Sherpa name. He is a genuine Sherpa, son of the famous hardy tribesmen. Perhaps I shall learn his full name during the coming weeks.

LP immediately took over; he obviously knew his business. First he inspected our cooking equipment and told us we needed one billycan for rice, one for curry, a kettle for tea and a frying pan. So, we can discard the rest for the trek. No tents: he arranges accommodation in villages. No stoves: he does the cooking on wood fires. At Namche Bazaar, his own village area, we can hire another porter to carry firewood up to base camp, and probably some small tents – if the hut is occupied we shall have to bivouac.

After lunch LP reappeared to help us do the shopping. He insisted on carrying the rucksack: good start! We bought 10lb porridge, 15lb sugar, 15lb rice, 15lb flour, soap, candles, toothpaste, matches, cooking oil, tea, and coffee. Between here and Namche Bazaar there is very little for sale, maybe some eggs and rice, so we have to carry everything. Fortunately the Sherpa carries 40lb of food, which leaves us about 15lb each to carry, plus personal gear.

Then we began packing everything into polythene bags and generally organising to be ready to leave on the 19th. Spent a while bartering watches on the black market; another interesting experience.

Because of our excitement and dashing about I never really noticed Kathmandu at all, save for the Ganesh Himal which was beautifully clear.

❧

John …

Dave came in with the news that our Sherpa would be arriving in an hour, having already been once while we were still in bed. We all immediately became jubilant and excited. When he arrived Dave and I talked to him and were immediately impressed with his quiet unassuming manner and cheerful ear-to-ear smile. He seemed a little young but said he had been to the South Col with both American and Indian expeditions. He told us he had been on Cho Oyu and Nanga Parbat as well. He was very proud of being a Sherpa. He took us to the room in which he was staying to show us some of his gear, and then we showed him some of ours. He said we didn't need tents or stoves, so that would be quite a saving in weight. He arranged to see us after his dinner to go shopping.

Dave and I accompanied the Sherpa (who told us to call him 'LP') to the market where we bought large quantities of porridge, cooking oil, sugar, flour, and rice. The rice was clearly not good quality and LP was most disgusted about it. After dumping all the food in our room he left us and we arranged to see him the next day. Les, Pam and I spent the rest of the afternoon packing some of the food. Towards sunset Pam and I went to buy a mirror and then went down to the footbridge across the river to look at the mountains, which were particularly clear that night.

Johnny ...   Today we met our Sherpa. He is a fabulous chap, aged only 23 and very small but he looks as strong as an ox and has loads of experience. He has been up to the South Col on Everest twice (26,600ft) and with the Germans on Dhaulagiri and Nanga Parbat. He has a fabulous sense of humour and a monstrous grin.

A late dinner but a good one. Les made an excellent curry and again produced some excellent rice. Cauliflower was only four pence. Tonight we had duck eggs again; chicken eggs for the morning. All the food is packed ready and we have our personal gear ready too.

Memories

Les ...   The preparations in Kathmandu were exciting, with the hiring of LP and Kaman and the purchase of baskets, pots and pans and foodstuffs (including the mysterious commodities 'pot-a-twos' and 'tom-a-twos', which turned out to be potatoes and tomatoes). I was also looking forward to seeing the big mountains.

Sunday 18th February

David ...   LP arrived early with a porter, Kaman, who for eight rupees a day will carry 80lb. First we had to buy him a basket at two rupees and a headband at one and a half rupees. He was then kitted up ready for off. After much arranging, repacking and sorting the Land Rover went off to the palace, leaving behind only the bare needs for our trek. All the foods, sugar, rice, cocoa, onions, tea, milk, meat bars, Horlicks concentrated meals, rum fudge and Complan for John and myself, were packed in polythene bags, courtesy of Mrs Smith (a good friend of my mother who had contacts with a factory that made a whole range of plastic bags).

After packing all our personal gear and anything the Sherpa and porter could not carry, I must have been carrying about 30-35lb, ample for a long walk. The 'employees' left and we went out for a pre-expedition dinner. Unfortunately, the Chinese 'Everest' restaurant was full, so we had an unsatisfactory chicken curry at The Opera. Bed was no relief from the excitement.

Spent most of the day preparing for the trek. Rang the Kumar up in the morning and arranged to leave the Land Rover at 5.00pm. LP went to look for a porter. Visited the post office to pick up mail and post some letters. Spent most of the afternoon packing food and in the evening went shopping with Pam to get her a hat – what a performance! LP didn't turn up at 6.00pm as arranged, so we went round to The Opera for a meal. On our return we met LP who was a little drunk. Nevertheless we eventually got sorted out with him and the porter in our room. The porter was to carry a huge load, poor devil – he hadn't even any shoes – and his wage was to be eight rupees (5s 4d) a day. A slightly restless night.

John …

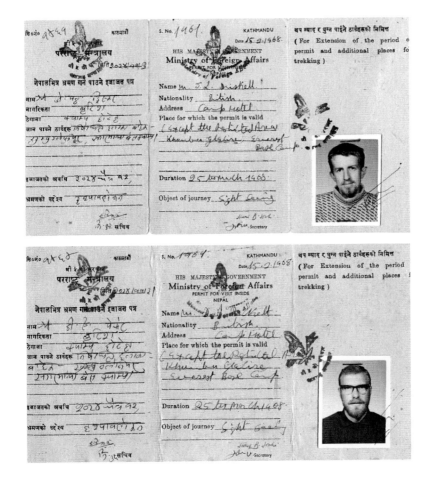

Visas stamped and cleared for "sight seeing".

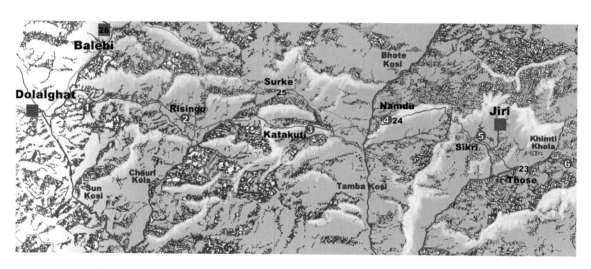

Our route across the foothills took six days between the 19th and 24th February.
(Outward route in red, return route in orange)
In 2010 we met Sherpa Ashok Rai, who remarked, "You know that route is very old route".

Chapter 4

Across the Foothills to the Khimti Kola

With our belongings packed in the Land Rover, which was parked safely inside the Royal Garages, we set off on our 300 mile trek. The loads we carried were as small as possible (though large enough at between 30-40lb) and apart from socks and underwear we took no spare clothes. Our diaries were locked away too and we used a notebook and pencil to record events, which we had to do in daylight or not at all.

We expected Johnny, a PE teacher, and John, an Outward Bound instructor, to be able to cope well with the physical demands of the coming trek. We were less sure about Pam and Les. But we knew the trek would be a huge challenge for David, despite the fact that he was a keen mountain walker at home. At the age of 11 he had contracted tuberculosis in his right hip joint and spent three years in Pinderfields Hospital in Wakefield. As a result of the disease he had a bone graft that fused his hip joint. As a consequence, he has no movement in his right hip and one leg is 5cm shorter than the other.

Monday 19th February, Day 1

At six in the morning we were ready for the off. LP and Kaman appeared and shouldered their loads. Few people moved in the

David ...

Getting off the bus in hot sun, at Dolalghat, to start our 300 mile trek. 19th February.

streets. The golden rays of sunrise set the wooden hamlets on fire and illuminated a million grains of pollen as we stepped sprightly along the muddy back streets.

The bus promised to leave at eight, not at seven as expected, so we left Kaman in charge of our bags and went for breakfast. We had to abandon all our rules of hygiene that, up to now, had prevented stomach upsets: we were in the hands of the gods. We had hardly eaten anything that we didn't cook ourselves since we left Barnsley. For the next few weeks we would have no control at all over levels of hygiene, as the cooking would be done by others and in primitive conditions. Tea and toast covered with pineapple jam were delicious.

Back at the bus, a crowd of peasants had gathered, their loads piled high on the roof. Women, their ears full of gold rings and with kukris (semi-curved metal knives) stuck in their belts, sat breast-feeding, crammed into the narrow seats.

Only a few yards after pulling away the bus 'put-putted' to a halt. The resident grease-monkey fell out and tinkered awhile to produce a spark of life. A mile down the road we had to stop at a garage to change a wheel. Then, after the fares were collected, we stopped for petrol. Next halt was beyond Bhadgaon at a village where LP bought hard-boiled eggs. The road wound along amid the fertile Kathmandu valley, then over the ridge to Dolalghat, where we got out.

Above us was the path, winding its way up the ridge. Before we started the pull uphill we had a meal of curried fish and rice in the roadside riverside café. It was hard work going uphill and the sun beat down as we pushed through several tiny hamlets. Sweat flowed in bucketsful. The only way I could see was to put my handkerchief, folded neatly, under the brim of my cap to stop the sweat from running down into my eyes. Several caravans of porters with enormous loads passed.

We had our first rest beneath a large Banyan tree, sharing the people's way of life. A small child aged about four or five had her baby brother slung on her back, just as the mothers do. Children very quickly have to share the family work. I felt unfit: my legs ached and my chest heaved. After two and half hours, we halted at a tiny village at about three o'clock. It was too far to the next reasonable halt, so fortunately we had a short day.

As we prepared for the evening meal, which LP cooked superbly, porters carrying long zinc water pipes began to arrive. Quickly they lit fires and cooked their meal of stiff cornflour paste and curry. They used kukris to shred the vegetables and chop the firewood. Kaman washed our socks while LP cooked. It seemed an ideal arrangement as we slumped in the late evening sun.

᪥

Mum's birthday. Woken at 6.10am by Dave. LP and the porter, *John …* Kaman, soon arrived, the latter still barefoot as he piled his little pack of personal belongings onto his huge basket. At the bus station we found we were three quarters of an hour early and so went for breakfast. We left Kaman in charge of our things. You felt sorry for him, but eight rupees a day must have seemed a reasonable deal to him. Pineapple jam, hot toast and tea and then back to the bus.

It was an eventful journey. We started with hardly anyone on board but we were soon full to capacity. The driver set off at 40mph over a very pot-holed road – although it was well engineered and not as steep as the Raj Path.

At Dolalghat we alighted in hot sun and had a curry in a rather dubious tea house. Then came the slog up a small rise, over a river by an iron bridge, and finally a great long 'graunch'. We all sweated like hell. Kaman and LP were a little way behind, having stopped to buy a headband. After two hours some of us were already suffering from blisters and LP said we would stop shortly in a 'house'.

Time about three o'clock. Good idea to have a short day. The house proved to be a fabulous hut with a fine view, and it gave us an insight into the life of the porters, who were sitting around wood fires cooking cornflour. Kaman washed our socks and LP cooked up a smashing curry. Les was a bit sick! We reckoned it was great being looked after by Sherpas. Got to bed early.

Spent the night at a hut on a hill above Dolalghat.

$\sim$

Johnny …   We were up by 6.00am, washed and beginning a hurried breakfast. LP arrived shortly afterwards and Kaman was at the door, waiting quietly to take on his load. Sacks were lifted and we were away, towards the waiting bus through sleeping Kathmandu. The streets were much quieter at this time of day and we saw only the bread boys gliding through the town with their steaming fresh 'Ashoka' bread. The ringing temple bells gave notice to all that at least some of the subjects had risen with the sun and were paying due homage.

The bus station, even at this hour, was busy with people everywhere; Sherpas, Buddhist Lamas, Tibetans going back to their homelands, piling onto buses of all shapes and sizes. Chaos reigned. Eventually LP found our bus and after the usual haggling over the fare we took our seats.

The crew of a bus comprises three men, the most important being the driver – on this occasion a swaggering individual who obviously regarded his ability as a God-given gift. The conductor was less gifted but seemed happy enough as he dispensed, apparently at random, a large array of multi-coloured tickets. The 'general help' completed the trio. His jobs were multitudinous. He sounded the horn, which was adequate enough on its own, but he supplemented it by banging the bus sides as we approached villages and towns. He acted as indicator board too: at each stop he leapt out and shouted wildly what our destination was. He also seemed to be some kind of mechanic, as he was well-endowed with grease and oil.

All the packing of goods on the roof was carried out by this lad of boundless energy. It was he who ran back to pick up the articles that broke loose on particularly rough stretches of road. At each long stop, some of them 20 minutes, he polished in vain the dilapidated coachwork, warned people of our departure and often found other jobs to do. Through all this he smoked, laughed, talked incessantly and obviously enjoyed every minute of his many occupations.

The passengers on the bus were a real mixture. For a start there were ourselves, a constant focus of attention in our climbing clothes and sun hats. Lamas sat, piously counting their prayer beads and hoping for a swift return to their mountain monasteries. Sherpas from the High Himalaya stood out from the Nepalese because some of their clothes were obviously cast-offs from expeditions to their mountains. Tibetans in their thick woollen robes, high boots and pigtails sat quietly and seemed rather amazed at the chaos around them. The Nepalese, their Indian blood in evidence, crashed about, shouted at one another, changed seats countless times, spat, coughed and were sick.

Motorised transport is a fairly recent thing in Nepal, and the inside of the bus was reminiscent of a rush-hour tube train, except for the coughing, spitting and vomiting. At one point as many as 60 people were packed into the tiny single-deck coach.

There are no level paths in Nepal. In one of the most difficult

'We sat under the tree of our first stop above Dolalghat with our eyes wide like saucers'. The bridge where we got off the bus can be seen below.

terrains in the world, paths go only up or down, and this one went up. For three and a half hours that day and for three hours the following day we went up and up without any change. Dolalghat stands at about 3000ft and during those two days we climbed slowly but surely to about 8000ft. As in the Alps, miles in this land are of no consequence and hours are the measure of distance. A village just a couple of miles across the valley may take four hours to reach.

The first impressions of walking are difficult to relate. At first you feel normal enough; after all, I've trudged many a path to many a mountain hut in Europe. Then slowly, yet irresistibly, the heat, the gradients, the dreadful condition of the surface and the seeming endless nature of your task impresses itself upon you. 'How can this go on for 30 days?' you ask yourself as you are forced to rest yet again. Of course, I am unfit. But what if my feet crack up? You can't just drop out and catch a bus. The only use they have for wheels in these cloud-reaching lands is for grinding. On and on, up and up, and then, at last, a final stop for the day, and peace.

Memories 2010

David ...   That morning when we walked along those smoke-filled streets I felt at the edge of my experiences, at the edge of my known world. I was filled with excitement. I was ready for the next stage of our

The porters quickly lit fires and cooked their meal of stiff corn flour paste.

expedition and to add to the rich and amazing experiences of our journey. I can still feel that anticipation of the completely unknown before us; there were no worries, just a kind of vacuum where knowledge and experience usually sit.

The bus wasn't ready and we went into a small room with tables and chairs. The toast and pineapple jam was just so tasty that we were intoxicated by it. We drew on the memories of that jam throughout the trek when our diet became monotonous. We promised ourselves that we would have a similar feast when we returned to Kathmandu.

In stark contrast was the riverside shack at Dolalghat and I felt very apprehensive. Throughout our journey we had been careful with the water and cooking to ensure we were healthy and avoided stomach and bowel problems. We sat on the bench seats and looked at each other. We were now in the hands of our Sherpa and the gods for the next month. The fish meal was tasteless and unappetising, an inauspicious start to having our food prepared for us.

We rested under a tree at our first stop above Dolalghat with our eyes wide as saucers. We felt close to the locals and their way of life. The first night was a good start. We had milky tea at the teashop near the path. We were so thirsty. The excitement of being in this remote spot alongside porters and their cooking fires made sleeping difficult.

❧

We had not gone more than a few hundred yards from the bus station before half of the locals were vomiting out of the windows. On arrival at Dolalghat, LP persuaded us to eat lunch in a small roadside restaurant. It consisted of curried fish bones and was the worst meal I have ever had, which didn't augur well for the rest of the trek.

Les ...

I found the walk to Namche Bazaar very hard. It was when we started walking, endlessly zigzagging upwards, that I began to wonder why I was there. Having not 'worn in' my new boots, I developed blisters on my heels. But prompt treatment cured them and I wore the same boots for the next 20 years without any problems. When we arrived at our first overnight stop, after much greater and more prolonged exertion than I had ever done before, the sudden cessation of hard physical effort caused me to vomit profusely, adding to my disenchantment.

Tuesday 20th February, Day 2

David … Up at 6.00am, after 11 hours in bed, to see a fantastic dawn. Golds and pinks flushed the distant range of snow-clad giants; each fang of the mountain jaw taking its turn to catch a ray of sunlight. At half past seven we set off, still uphill. Far below, the terraced hillsides spread right down to the river valley where villages, tiny white blocks, clung tightly to the banks.

Saw a corn mill powered by water; mechanisation is very rare. Saw a buffalo being milked – the first time I have seen milking since home. Saw a woman pounding grain in a hollow log, another winnowing the separated husk from the grain. Buffalos are used to pull ploughs wherever the terrace is large enough. In the silence the shouts of the ploughmen sound much the same as Dad when he ploughed with horses.

By 5.00pm, when we arrived at Risingo, we were exhausted after trekking uphill most of the day. I much prefer the uphills because I can maintain a steady plod; downhill is hard work for me. We climbed down to a lush river valley, rich in rhododendron trees and mosses, thronging with strange bird calls, before a very steep ascent that just about finished us all.

LP found us a home on the veranda of a Nepalese house. My sense of smell seems more acute: I passed a man eating an orange that I could smell a full 50 yards before I saw him; I notice traces of cows and goats that must have passed earlier. Kaman, our slim, waif-like porter, just goes on and on. Johnny's feet are very badly blistered, otherwise all well but tired. From the veranda we could see peaks commanding the northern horizon. Our 'hostess' wandered around with a basket cradle slung on her headband. By swinging her backside she rocked the basket whenever her baby murmured.

During the evening there was a fantastic thunderstorm. Lightning played among the distant peaks, running its forked tongue over the white teeth. Rain penetrated the thatch, so we climbed inside our large polybags. Les went inside complaining bitterly about the rain. We were in bed by seven.

Off at the crack of dawn with beautiful views of mountains. The uphill slope continued, but fortunately we were in the shade at this time of day. Les and Dave set off first and half an hour later Pam, Johnny and I followed. When we got to the top of the first slope we found there were many more to go. They went on for three hours, easing off towards the top. Dinner stop was a great relief and LP cooked another 'ace' curry. Between us we had 15 cups of tea and one glass of milk that cost one and a half rupees (1s 0d).

John …

It was painful restarting and we were soon caught up by a Swiss chap we had met at the Secretariat in Kathmandu, his wife and a Sherpa. There was a long level stretch and then a steep descent. Lost Pam for a short time and didn't know whether she was in front or behind. We followed a river valley for some time and then there was the long, hot, final 'graunch' uphill.

At Risingo we were to sleep on the veranda of a house with a view straight across the valley. LP turned up trumps again with buffalo curry and cocoa, and he also brewed two good cuppas before our meal. Kaman arrived a quarter of an hour after us, looking as fresh as a daisy. It was proving to be a great 'natural' life, being near to nature and requiring great effort, but well worth experiencing. It was funny to think that we were on one of the country's arterial communications routes. We passed a large group of porters carrying iron pipes today..

Spent the night at Risingo.

Memories 2010

As he did every morning, LP cooked us porridge and Dave and I had Complan scattered over it. The others refused Complan because of the taste.

John …

We hadn't anticipated employing a porter but LP insisted that it was necessary and although our finances were not extensive, we agreed. We didn't really have much choice as we needed him to carry most of the supplies.

Kaman was to be paid less than a Sherpa and he was to provide his own food rather than eat ours along with LP. We were a little uneasy with this arrangement, with its overtones of hierarchy and class, but it seemed to be the way of the land and our finances would be further stretched if we sought to override it. Reluctantly we went along with it.

Our food was certainly not lavish but Kaman's was very basic. He ate tsampa, which is roasted barley flour, and he needed some fluid to enable him to make it into a sort of dumpling. Usually he begged some tea from us but occasionally we would give him curry sauce, to his obvious delight. I noticed that his breakfast was a couple of handfuls of rolled rice, which he ate from his jacket pocket as we walked along.

At night he just lay on the floor on his back and carefully put his scarf over himself to sleep. His was a life of such simplicity, carried out with such dignity and lack of complaint, that our admiration and respect for him grew as the days went by.

৵

David …   Good old Les – when the rain started to penetrate and drip he was hurt, angry and fed up. He was not prepared to suffer and fought his way into the house, dragging his sleeping bag to a drier place. I never saw where he slept, but it became such a laugh next morning when he emerged ready for the banter that would add to the 'Legends of Les', though he was still a little grumpy about the rain. The joys of trekking clearly eluded him.

Wednesday 21st February Day 3

David …   An 'easy' but slow start to the day that involved going downhill to yet another deep, rushing river valley. A lunch of pancakes made a change from rice and curry. LP is very efficient; he sees to our every need, especially our great need for tea. Kaman is always hovering around to help him.

Johnny's feet are very bad and he could hardly walk at lunch time. In the village he bought plimsolls to try in place of his crippling boots. John and I feared this would happen, but Johnny had insisted that his untested boots would be fine. He'd only climbed two crags in them. It could spoil the whole trek.

After sweating up to a high col we contoured then dropped down for about an hour to Katakuti. Again we are on a veranda, this time with animals to keep us company. Goats and chickens wander freely over the dirty straw mats our hosts had put down for us. Just as we arrived, another mighty thunderstorm broke in a display of power among the hills that made the peaks in the far north seem to tremble.

The scenery changed little, save for our first rhododendron forest. These are not pretty bushes, but tall, stout trees. Some are in flower but generally they are just budding.

We popped into a corn mill to find two men beaming away as they fed grain into the hole in the middle of the upper grindstone. Flour spilled out between the two wheels to fall in heaps on the dusty floor. Why had they not devised some better, more efficient, cleaner method of collecting the flour? Cherry trees are in blossom around the village.

Tonight's house is a real education in Nepalese life. Downstairs is the animal house, plus fireplace. The fireplace has an open wood fire with stones to rest the pots on. Dogs, goats, hens and tiny chickens run among the open spaces between the firewood. Smoke fills the whole room, filtering out where it can. It creeps upstairs, fills that room, then escapes through the thatch. Initiative could devise a chimney – even the Anglo-Saxons had a hole in the roof.

A clear warm night was spoiled by a dog barking on and on. We all had a go at stoning it. With each successful hit it merely changed note.

❧

Pam and I set off last again, starting the day with a steep descent *John …* and a rickety trestle bridge. A steep but fairly short climb followed and we caught the others up at the top. The track then contoured along a valley to a little village at its head. Here we had a delightful shady dinner break and LP cooked some delicious pancakes. I put my plimsolls on afterwards to try them out and found them a great comfort. We passed a little school house where the class and teacher posed for a photo.

I felt fine on the next long steep stretch but towards the top, after waiting for Pam, my ankle began to hurt. Along the top the clouds began to gather. Just before the col we sampled some 'chang' the native

Packing our bags before leaving Risingo. It had rained in the night and our polythene bags have been hung to dry.

hooch. The slope down the other side never seemed to end and I was going very slowly with Pam. Just before reaching Katakuti it started to rain, with flashes of lightning. Very tired that night, but nevertheless it was great just sitting relaxing in the shelter of the veranda with rain pouring off the thatched roof and thunder rattling around the valleys.

Spent the night at Katakuti.

Memories 2010

David ... We had tried many times to get Johnny to break his boots in but he didn't. He was always so self-confident and sure there would be no problems. His feet were such a mess that I really felt we would have to give up or leave him in a village until his feet recovered. I was ready to find somewhere where he could stay. I had to walk on alone for a while. But he battled on and when he began to walk in John's sandals he started to recover and he showed strength and determination to keep going until the raw flesh began to heal. But his feet remained a mess for most of the trek.

Johnny's self-confidence was a real asset but sometimes it caused him *John …* to come unstuck, as it did on this occasion with his boots. I remember just three months before we set off, we were climbing Troutdale Pinnacle Direct in Borrowdale with Alan Roberts, one of my colleagues from Ullswater Outward Bound School. Alan was a good climber and subsequently climbed Changabang in the Karakorum Range on the China-Pakistan border.

The crux of our Lake District climb involved a very thin and committing move. Alan spent a good while attempting it before giving up, then I had a go and couldn't do it either. Johnny went straight up, made the committing move and fell off! I can picture now his body falling past us and shooting down a gully before coming to a halt as the rope pulled taught. He had a nasty 'puncture' wound on his stomach. It could so easily have been the end of his dreams of going to Everest.

&

Notwithstanding the incredible beauty of the country through *Les …* which we passed, I spent a lot of time planning and searching for possible places in villages where I could stay and await the return of the other four. In the first few days it was only the fear of appearing 'wimpish' that kept me going.

Thursday 22nd February, Day 4

A third magnificent dawn revealed the startling bulk of the Jugal *David …* Himal. Yellows and greys brought shapes and shadows to life. There were no reds, just one pillar of gold that climbed from the hills onto the clouds and became the sun. No fuss, no excitement, it just rose into the day.

First a long, slow, downhill trek through richly scented pine woods to the big river, fed by the snows of the Jugal. To cross the river we had to use a very narrow suspension bridge that swayed with every step. I was quite scared. A local woman following us would not cross. She climbed down the bank and waded across the fast-flowing river. After climbing uphill to a village the path contoured round to another

....we had to use a very narrow suspension bridge that swayed with every step.

village, shaded by enormous mango trees. A contouring path is fine, but this one had many ups and downs, which was a nuisance.

After chapattis and omelette we had a long, long 'downhill' to the swift river that filled the whole valley, fed by the mighty Gauri Sanker. Its bulk was beyond comprehension. What will the truly big ones be like? Beneath a deep blue sky a good bridge crossed the green glacier waters. Many people were gathered around the bridge. There was a band making a cacophony, rather like half a dozen children trying to imitate Chris Barber (who had a very popular jazz band in the 1950s). A long thrape followed that: a long, long 'uphill': sweat, hot sun, perspiration, hot sun. Two hours before I rested though, so I must be getting fitter.

Met many Tibetans with their friendly "Namaste" ("Greetings"). They wear thick black robes like cloaks, thick trousers and woven calf-length boots with a leather moccasin sole. Many people ask about my limp. I don't suppose they see many sahibs with a limp; for ease I usually signify I have had a broken bone.

Namdu was our home for the night. We met a Sherpa there who turned out to be Joe Brown's Sherpa on Kangchenjunga (first climbed by a British expedition, including Brown, in 1955). I said JB is the best British rock climber and he replied: "Him like a monkey" with appropriate actions to show Joe on rock.

LP established us on a veranda between a hand-powered corn mill and a pivoted corn-masher powered by foot. We had a brew of sweet tea that we gulped down as quickly as possible, regardless of heat. Full of rice and curry, and after a big wash, we were in bed by seven o'clock. There's nothing like a healthy life with plenty of exercise, food and sleep.

᪶

From our beds there was a smashing view across the valley of snow-covered peaks. Pam, Johnny (with very bad feet) and I set off half an hour after the others – yet again. A long, slow descent getting very steep towards the river, which was crossed by a very rickety suspension bridge; I found it quite nerve-racking to cross. This was followed by a short, steep climb and then level, slightly undulating ground across terraced fields to our dinner stop. Chapattis and omelette – great, but Oh! What nectar was the tea! Les said that he was getting "cheesed off" – a bit early to be feeling like that with 200-or-so miles still in front of you.

Further steep descent down wooded hillsides to a large river. We caught a magnificent view of the high peak of Gauri Sanker, enormous above high foothills. At the bottom were large crowds of porters and some very friendly Tibetans. We had a cooling wash in the river, reluctant to face the steep hill ahead. Then we started steadily upwards, following Kaman along a by-track. It was the steepest uphill 'graunch' so far and the highest.

Now walking together (apart from Dave, who was some way in front), we plodded through the hot forest with only two stops. Pam did particularly well. As we rounded the corner at the top we got a refreshing breeze and good hill views. The worst was over and we had only another half an hour to go to Namdu. We arrived there quite early and had a fine hut for the night. Took a six-minute walk to the water supply and had a good 'bath'. Another great meal and then our Swiss friend came for a talk. We seemed to be travelling parallel to him.

Spent the night in Namdu at an altitude of 4,724ft.

Memories 2010

The paths were well worn by centuries of Sherpas and porters travelling the hills from village to village. Some areas were paved with silica rock but mostly the path was worn sandy earth that I stared at endlessly to ensure a secure footfall. This was no place to twist an ankle or knee. I talked about that possibility and what we would do. The suggestion was to leave the person in the nearest village house to recover. A break would have been much more severe and would have needed porters to carry the person back to the road. I did slip on an

*Gauri Sankar
from just below
Kirantichap.*

icy root several days later and wore my knee bandage for a while. I worried for about an hour until it settled down and I walked it off.

As I walked and stared at the paths I was always captured by the mica crystals that sparkled in the sunshine. When I chose my souvenir rocks from Base Camp I carefully chose one that sparkled.

The monotony of walking, plodding up hill and down, allowed my imagination to move freely. It was as though I had a slide projector in my head – a slide would drop of some memory and my daydreams would focus on that for a while. Something like a camp in the Cairngorms or my Dad milking. Then suddenly another slide would drop and the dream changed. I had two recurring daydreams: one was to change to primary school teaching, the other, stranger, was to run a book shop on Market Hill in Barnsley. I planned the shop and the coffee bar with tables and magazines. I would get mother to cook scones and coffee buns, etc. It was interesting how my brain occupied itself while concentrating intensely on the ground around my feet, but where the bookshop came from I have no idea, though I can still see the vision clearly.

John ... As we sheltered from the sun for lunch, Les came in to join us, red in the face and mopping his brow with a handkerchief. It was at this point he uttered the now famous line: "We've invented the wheel, we've invented the plane and here we are walking 300 bloody miles." Though we all laughed, I felt sorry for him. He could have stayed in Kathmandu but the thought of a month on his own seemed less attractive than the alternative. I walked with him up the long steep hill to Namdu and tried to lift his spirits. Personally, I had found the walking fairly easy; it was more or less what my job had been the previous year.

At the same lunch stop, Dave hung his sweat-soaked handkerchief to dry on a bush whilst we rested. I remember him suddenly jumping to life and shouting out like the Barnsley farmer his father was. I looked up just in time to see the last remnants of his handkerchief disappearing into a cow's mouth. On a trek such as this, it was a more serious loss than you might imagine.

∽

The countryside was incredibly beautiful, with its neat terraces, flowers, picturesque villages and friendly smiling people, but I found the endless slog tedious. To help bear this and to pass the time I tried to go through as much as I could remember of Beethoven's symphonies in my head.

Some children pose for the camera at our lunch stop.

Les …

Friday 23rd February, Day 5

Just after 5.00am, in the dark, two men arrived to use the corn-masher, used for de-husking rice. We had to be up before LP produced tea.

Most of the morning was spent grinding uphill through rhododendron woods. The hill was too steep for me to swing my leg through, so I was slower than usual. Far behind, we could see our stop of a day-and-a-half ago, although it seemed much longer ago than that.

David …

My memory of the various paths and views is dulled by the constant need to concentrate on every step. No surface is good enough to allow me to look around occasionally; I just stare at the mica dust and the mica rocks, all sparkling in the sun.

On the top of the ridge, at about 8,000ft, our hopes of seeing Gauri Sankar were dashed. Clouds clung to the whole range of peaks and nothing was visible. Far below, a beautiful river led away. To reach it there was a steep descent which really pulled on my thighs. For the first time ever, I could feel the muscles in my right thigh. We met a couple having great trouble trying to bring down a calf; obviously the ascent had exhausted it. It kept flopping down and refusing to go further. (Johnny had seen them at the top – they were Buddhists – collect a rhododendron leaf and tap each person and the calf on the head before putting the leaf on the Chorten – a Buddhist place of worship – amid the prayer flags.)

When I reached the bottom of the valley I found LP negotiating for a billycan of buffalo meat for four rupees. On the opposite hillside a huge team of porters crept up towards Jiri. Resting places on the tracks are walls with ledges set just high enough for the porters to rest their baskets without having to bend to release the pack or to lift it. All the porters carry a T-shaped walking stick that they prop under their basket when they want a rest mid-way between these specially built walls.

We stayed in a very poor 'rest house'. The owners were very uncooperative. Kaman, the hero, had to chop the firewood. Johnny and I slept on the small veranda alongside two dogs and a host of chickens and a broody hen. Johnny's feet look terrible. A good job John brought his sandals or Johnny would not have been able to go on. Les seems to be hating every minute. He was not too keen to come and I don't think he realised just what 'walking' could involve. I'm loving it, though my feet are very tired tonight.

Woken in the morning by a bloke who wanted to pound grain in the corner next to Dave's bed. I set off with Pam but Johnny walked with her after the water temple. The first section was long and flat and enabled us to get warmed up, then the path steadily ascended to a little village, by which time I had passed everyone else. I waited for Johnny and Pam as everybody passed me and we took the stiff climb to the lunch spot. Not as nice as usual as there were too many flies. Nevertheless LP cooked yet another ace curry. After dinner we followed the very exposed track that crossed a stream and then climbed very steeply through woods. Met the Tibetans again – great people.

The ascent eased but rather than coming to an end, it continued on up to a col with many 'rhodydodies', and then up further to another col where we caught up with the others and had a rest. There should have been good views of Gauri Sankar from here but we caught only a glimpse through the cloud. A steep down slope followed, which Johnny and I took at speed to save the pain.

By the river I bathed my feet as LP bought some buffalo meat from a passer-by. It was very pleasant there with the sparkling stream, green grass and cumulus clouds – it could easily have been in the Lakes. This was the first time we had seen no terraced fields. The Swiss party went on to Jiri but we followed the valley down, on a very pleasant walk to a little village. Pam fell on her face and cut her lip. Not such a good spot to sleep, with three of us in a tent. LP didn't seem satisfied but didn't feel like moving on. Washed vest in the stream, dhobi style.

Spent the night at Sikri, altitude 6,168ft.

8 miles; 3,675ft ascent; 2,231ft descent.

Memories 2010

The paths we walked were the trade routes of rural Nepal and porters carried all sorts of commodities from place to place. We passed some carrying long zinc pipes between two of them, heading for a destination over 90 miles away. Tibetans walked across the mountains to trade in India. We sometimes passed them. When we were downwind we could often detect their approach by a distinctive odour. This was shortly followed by ear-to-ear smiles as they approached to greet us with the traditional 'Namaste'. What lovely, happy, cheerful people they were. On one occasion a group was accompanied by a small boy about four years old and LP told us that they, including the boy, had walked 200 miles to India to trade and were now on their way home, a round trip of 400 miles.

Saturday 24ᵗʰ February, Day 6

David ... I slept well alongside the menagerie, which finally woke me as they fluttered over my sleeping bag. One dog messed Johnny's polybag.

A long leisurely walk along the river bank to Those. It is the first proper village since Dolalghat. It has narrow streets, paved with stone slabs, shops and terraced houses. It looks extremely old, like pre-fire 17ᵗʰ Century London. Down by the river, which had very high banks, the women beat washing on the rocks. Again there seems to be a complete lack of enterprise to help themselves. Women have to go down the steep and awkward banks to the river for water and to wash clothes. Steps would be invaluable, as would some sort of set-up for washing. But there's absolutely nothing being done.

In the beautiful valley we find eggs are cheap – four for one rupee – so we had curry with a fried egg on top. Superb! A woman with the most horrible persistent cough was slumped in the corner of the room we ate in. TB, no doubt.

'Two hours later Pam and I arrived at the first Sherpa house'.

We bought some rice. What a difference from the Kathmandu varieties; this is much coarser and not so sweet. Fancy being able to notice a difference in rice; still, it makes a change from King Edwards!

This four-year-old boy had just walked 400 miles from India, and he's still smiling!

Farther along the valley we had to decide whether to stop early or push on. Still feeling quite fresh, we decided to make it to the first Sherpa house and split the enormous hill in front of us into two stints. It was the first of three huge ridges we must cross. I nearly fell into the river before deciding to use the bridge. We made it to the house quite late but not feeling too bad; muscles much better; all feeling happier.

The Sherpa house is quite different from Nepalese houses. Animals, cows only, still inhabit the ground floor. The house has stout stone walls and the roof is covered in wooden shingles held down by rocks. We are sleeping in a straw-filled barn. In the house is a complete mixture of possessions: a rifle, pictures of Liz Taylor, climbing boots, copper bowls, chests, suitcases, a 'Christmas' paper ball hung from the roof. There is a letter from our hosts' son who is serving with the Gurkhas in Hong Kong; he is in England now. It made me feel quite remote – their son in England, me here in the remote Himalaya. The day closed with a fantastic sunset.

∽

W e started off on a beautiful walk along the shady river valley, crossed the river and started uphill. We soon reached the top and LP said that it was very easy after this. Walked downhill to the main river valley and stopped at a beautiful spot on its banks. I washed my handkerchief as we took a short rest. After half an hour upstream, we stopped in Those, the largest village we had encountered since we set off. There we had lunch. LP cooked while we waited upstairs for the 'nosh', in a quaint room with beams of sunlight shining through the gaps in the roof and patterns of smoke drifting through them. After

John ...

Those, the largest village we passed through.
'… It looks extremely old, like 17th Century London' before the Great Fire'.

the meal we stocked up with some more food and bought a kitchen towel before moving on upstream. Great to have an easy day!

After an hour LP asked if we wanted to continue up the hillside. We did, and so started a very steep climb that fortunately began to ease off higher up. Two hours later Pam and I arrived at the Sherpa house (the first one we've stayed at). It was completely different from Nepalese houses. We were high up the mountainside and had a good view of a lightly snow-covered hill. Inside the house it was very dark with low beams. The Sherpas sat around the fire in the middle of the floor. There was a vicious dog outside.

Spent the night at 'Sherpa House', altitude 7,743ft.

8.75 miles; 2,887ft; 1,181ft descent.

Memories 2010

David … The house in Those was very dark and the room overlooked the village street. We sat on the floor with backs to the wall and that poor woman coughed in the most disturbing manner, which left her completely debilitated. I was quite frightened of the disease and our contact with it so it was pleasure to find the open fresh air again.

The Khimti Khola river. 'We walked downhill to the main river valley and stopped at a beautiful spot on its banks'.

Kaman carrying his huge load using a headband and walking as he always did, barefoot!
The village of Namdu is on the hillside to the right of the tree.

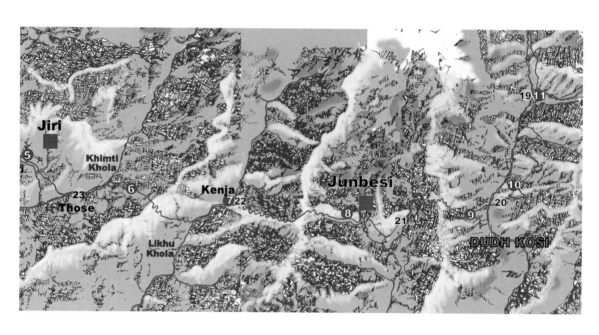

The great 'graunch' across the three mighty ridges, accomplished in as many days, between 25th and 27th February

Chapter 5

Over Three Great Ridges into the Namche Valley

Sunday 25th February, Day 7

A deep frost greeted us at 6.00am. High on the top of the col, we could see a few peaks over the intermediate hills, glistening against the egg-shell-blue sky. We went into the house for breakfast. Inside was just as dark as it was last night. It can't be healthy to live in darkness always filled with smoke.

David ...

After a steady climb we descended through woods until we stopped to have lunch near a large stupa (a mound-like structure containing Buddhist relics)) with the all-seeing eyes of Lord Buddha fading beneath the bleached paint. Before plunging down to the valley bottom we crossed a flat valley where farmers were busy ploughing; in other fields whole families hacked away at the surface with a hoe-cum-spade. Going down steep descents gives the knees some work as you hold back against gravity.

At Kenja we faced the second big ridge and we had to decide whether to continue up and on or to take an early rest. Kaman felt he could not make the next rest place before dark so we stayed there. A small market was in progress in the boulder-strewn village. Three valleys meet here and the floods have pushed up a boulder mass upon which these people live and cultivate a crop between the rock piles. Half a dozen people were selling odds and ends – no more than a basketful – with a crowd hanging around who were amused to see us.

Our veranda was again small for five, so we put up the tent.

Above: A glimpse of high hills through flower-filled forest.

Below: The Bhudist Chorten at Barrikharga (Bhandar).

Above: David 'tops out' on the pass over to the Likhu Khola valley.

Below Left: A view from the trail of terraced fields and settlements.

Below Right: A small market was in progress in the boulder-strewn village … with a crowd hanging around who were all amused at seeing us'.

Being in cheap chicken country we bought one. Between us we picked a large cockerel, which LP curried. He divided up the bird with swift blows from his kukri knife, bones and all. Picking out pieces in the dark and eating them was not an enjoyable feast.

❧

A cold frosty night. We began the day following a gently rising track through shady forests with the scents of pine and perfumed shrub pervading the frosty air. Once on the col we got views of snow-covered peaks and the tip of Gauri Sankar. We could also see a high distant col over which we would have to travel, not a pleasant thought. We made a quick, sunny descent to Barikharga (marked as Bhandar on maps, though this is undoubtedly what LP called it) for a pancake dinner.

John …

Off by 11.30am, down a gently descending track that after a mile or so, dropped very steeply to the Likhu Khola Valley. It turned rather cloudy as we followed the valley up to Kenja. Here everyone was feeling a little tired and the next 'kipping' spot was four hours away. We decided to carry on if Kaman agreed, but he said it was not possible so we found a house for the night. Les and Pam's faces were classic mixtures of joy and relief on hearing this news.

We had to pitch tent again. An early start was necessary the next day, when we should be able to climb in the shade. LP bought a chicken for us at eight and a half rupees. He didn't dare kill it as he said he had once killed a sheep and had nightmares. Kaman did the honours.

I was pleasantly surprised at our progress, after my initial depression when I thought we were slacking with this second easy day. Washed some socks. It was good to have an early stop for a change. Hot chicken curry for supper.

Spent the night at Kenja, altitude 5,249ft.

7.75 miles; 1,575ft ascent; 3,937ft descent; (Crossed pass 8,875ft).

❧

Memories 2010

David …   Oh, it was great fun picking out the bantam-sized cockerel for our meal. Kaman smiled as he caught it and killed it. When it was plucked and gutted it was chopped into quite large cubes using a kukri. I think I realised then that, once in the stew, it might not be such a delightful chicken. When it was served I lay in the darkness of the house using my spoon to eat the rice. The chicken had become bony, sinewy, skin-covered lumps of tough meat. I did my best but I quietly disposed of most of it. It was probably one of the worst meals of my life because it was eaten in darkness. It was impossible to see what I was eating until I crunched on the bones or the gristle. My stomach found it repulsive and I couldn't swallow it.

Monday 26th February, Day 8

David …   We had a poor night's sleep because of a dog barking incessantly. In these small communities the night is filled with barking, howling dogs. The family rose at about 4.00am, rushing about with fire-brand torches that were spitting sparks. At five the woman came out to begin grinding maize flour. She squats on the ground, turning the top stone with one hand, feeding in the sweetcorn with the other. The flour spills out onto the dirty floor to be swept up later. We ate porridge, as usual, with Complan scattered on top, and we gazed up the valley at the dawn spectacle. Strange how you watch the light grow but never realise that suddenly it is light.

Began our uphill at 6.35am, our earliest start yet. It was very hard going for two hours until we reached the Sherpa house that was the rest house involved in last night's decision. We could have made it. Over a superb curry lunch we gazed at the distant foothills, covered in pines and dressed with snow.

Two hours later we reached the ridge, our highest yet. From there we traversed for one hour in deep snow before dropping down through the dense pine and rhododendron forest. It was a sunless, cold and damp descent amongst the trees where mosses and lichens flourished. On the top (at 3,530m, about 10,000ft), we stared into a deep

valley, completely free of human influence because of its steep rocky sides.

Kaman actually put plimsolls on that were ten sizes too big for him so that he could cross our first patch of Himalayan snow. We met two Japanese who were just returning from Base Camp.

Tonight's Sherpa house is next to a temple. We slept in the ante-room to a huge prayer wheel that rings a bell when spun. Many prayer flags and inscriptions filled the walls.

༄

We have now been trekking for a week. Got up early and watched the sun rise over the white peaks at the head of this steep-sided valley. We were off very early and straight away we were on the uphill, very steep with zigzag after zigzag, on and on through the morning. At one point we passed LP's 'second father' (we had no idea what LP meant when he referred to his 'second father' – perhaps it was his step-father). After two hours' hard work we were relieved to see our dinner-time stopping place a little lower than we had expected. It was only 9.30am.

After lunch we continued the stiff 'graunch' uphill (I had to go back for my handkerchief at one point). Up and up again, onto the top of the ridge, which we then followed upwards to the mist level where everyone was waiting for Pam and me. We ate the boiled eggs we had bought and they were delicious.

The next section was a traverse across the snowy side of the ridge

Above Left: The traverse to the Lamjura Pass, where 'twisted, moss-covered the trees on either side, through which the path formed a tunnel'.

Above Right: Taking a rest by the prayer flags on the top of the Lamjura Pass the highest on route to Everest.

John ...

to another col. Kaman's shoes were too big for him and as he prodded them with a perturbed look on his face, LP showed obvious amusement. I lent him mine, which fitted quite well. We crossed the snow, sensing its strange wintry atmosphere. There were twisted, moss-covered trees at each side, through which the path formed a tunnel. Surprisingly, it took an hour to cross and I shot on ahead because the glare was hurting my eyes.

At the col I sat down by the prayer flags outside a Buddhist temple and gazed down over a beautiful valley, very Swiss-like in appearance, with no terracing but forested and interspersed with grass slopes. Then down through the snow-slush forests where we stopped for a chat with some Japanese trekkers and had a look at their map. We took it easy after this to our stopping place just before Junbesi. It was a good spot and we slept on a balcony next to a prayer-wheel. We found the Swiss were only just in front. We all seem much fitter now.

Spent the night at Tragdobuk Monastery near Junbesi, altitude 9,383ft.

8.25 miles; 6,299ft ascent; 2,231ft descent. (Crossed pass at altitude 11,581ft)

Memories 2010

John ... This day we climbed continuously for over 6,000ft and reached the snow line just before the pass. Kaman had asked for an advance on his pay so that he could buy some shoes in Kathmandu market and this was the first time he had got them out, to walk through the snow. It seems he hadn't realised that shoes came in sizes and he hadn't tried them on! They were many sizes too big. I lent him mine as I had changed into boots.

Tuesday 27th February, Day 9

David ... Dawn of the finest gold: again there were no reds, only creams and gold to daylight. The lethargic ones are no better at rising and always cause a small delay as they have to catch up with their packing!

Junbesi is a large collection of solid houses set deep in the valley

bottom. At the head of the valley is Numbur Himal, which LP climbed with a Japanese team. On the climb out of the valley we found a new plant, a shrub that smells strongly of lilac. It has a sort of ball of pink or white flowers, similar to a lilac.

As we rounded the hill we were met by the fantastic sight of big mountains rising before us, possibly to heights of 20,000ft to 24,000ft. On the extreme right was Ama Dablam. Their fluted snow faces hid the really big ones. Broody clouds rushed in to hide the scene long before we reached the valley bottom.

After lunch it was hard work to reach the next high ridge, the last of the big three. From its cold top we could see little of what was to come. As we dropped down we passed the temporary residences of herdsmen with their herds of yak-cow cross. We bought eggs from a couple who were squatting by the path, miles from anywhere. They probably sit there all day waiting for customers. We got 28 eggs for eight rupees. Rounding the next spur brought the mighty Namche Valley and the Dudh Kosi into view.

Our night's stop was in a half-built rough timber house. We were made most welcome and the man put down planks on the bare soil floor for us to sleep on. With the promise of superb views in the morning, we went to bed at our usual hour of 7.00pm.

'… unfortunately we knew no names but took photos nevertheless'. The Everest Range appears beyond the Tragsindo La, the final pass to the Dudh Kosi Valley.

ക

'… We rounded a corner and beheld a magnificent view of Numbur Himal.'

John … It was a beautiful morning as we walked along the mountainside to Junbesi. We rounded a corner and beheld a magnificent view of Numbur Himal (also known as Shorong Yul Lha 6,958m, 22,831ft). LP had been to its summit and he pointed out the camps. Our route then went down slightly to the village of Junbesi, across the river and up through pine forests until we came to a stream, where Pam and I stopped to do some washing. After that, the path contoured along a beautiful mountainside. As we rounded the hill we gained a fantastic view of the Himalaya at quite close range; fluted ice walls and towering white peaks in profusion. Unfortunately we knew no names but took photographs nevertheless. We carried on traversing throughout the morning, eyes fixed on the mountains that were slowly clouding over.

Dinner was cold and we ate it inside a Sherpa house. After dinner we took an hour to get down to the river bed and then Johnny and I made it up the next col in 40 minutes, and we ate rum fudge. LP lit a fire, as it was now cold and cloudy, and we waited for the others. Pam, Johnny and I descended slowly.

LP bought 28 cheap eggs from a peasant on the path side. We hoped they would prove to be a tasty addition to our diet. It was a longer descent than we had expected and it took us two hours to reach the bottom. At our night stop we sat round the fire to warm up and

68

our Sherpa hosts put down boards over the mud floor for us to sleep on. Much warmer at night, but very low cloud.

Spent the night at a half-built hut near Phuleli, altitude 6,299ft.

13 miles; 3,018ft ascent; 6,298ft descent. (Crossed pass 10,075ft)

Memories 2010

I remember the couple huddled by the path with a basketful of eggs, *David …* hoping for passing trade. We looked from the high ridge through the trees and wondered where possible customers might come from. I can't remember how we then carried 28 eggs safely to our next cooking stop.

Oh, the rum fudge! What a ritual its consumption became. We were rationed to eat it only every three days and we had to decide at what point on that day we would share the special treat. The small square was placed on the tongue and allowed to melt and the burst of flavour was ecstatic, hallucinogenic and very short lived. The shadow of the next three rum-fudgeless days then hovered over us for a few minutes.

We had boiled sweets, which were welcome, but although each lasted longer than the fudge, they were never real competitors. I dreamed of the flavour of rum fudge. We talked of the flavour. We craved the flavour and talked about buying huge quantities and gorging on it when we returned to England. I have never tasted it since eating the last pack on the trek.

The first day or two we had rum fudge every day, but when we *John …* divided what we had into 28 (to last the whole trek) and then into five equal portions, the amount we actually got was so small it was hardly worth having, so we agreed to make it a three-day treat. It was still a pretty small portion, but utterly divine! (The rum fudge was in expedition packs bought from Benjamin Edgingtons in Manchester)

We relied totally on LP to find the route as we had no maps and our only way of knowing the names of mountains and villages was to ask him. Of course we didn't know which language he was using and we didn't know if we had heard him correctly. We wrote his words phonetically and there was considerable room for error. We recorded Numbur Himal in our diaries as Lumba Himal because that is what we thought LP said. It was years before we found maps which made us aware of the mistake.

'...Dawn of the finest gold ...'.

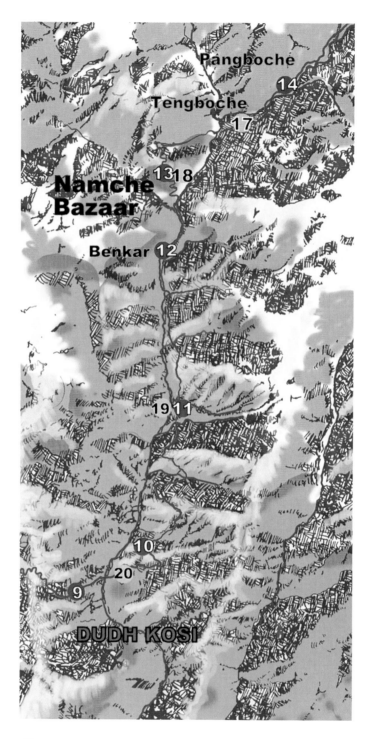

Four days to Namche Bazaar: mile after mile, ridge after ridge, valley after valley

Chapter 6

Up the Dudh Kosi
to Namche Bazaar

Wednesday 28th February, Day 10

We had a disturbed night because rain began to fall at about 2.00am. It penetrated the roof easily and dripped constantly onto my polybag protection. The stupid cockerel, cooped just above my head, began to crow at 4.00am, very regularly, continuing until we got up at 6.00am. Our promise of views was shattered, as deep cloud filled the valleys and light rain fell all morning.

David …

Down through forest we went to meet the waters that flow from almighty big mountains. What a valley it was: rich in life, with extremely high steep sides. Amazing that all the valleys are water cut, not glaciated. For lunch we tried to stay at a Sherpa's we had met yesterday – Rai Sherpa who showed us a scar where a Japanese sword had gone through his leg – but his wife wouldn't entertain us, so we moved next door.

Next we made a steep ascent. I was using my new super calf muscles and in the very humid valley this made me really sweat. From the col a large zigzag path led up the other side of the valley – our target for today. Two hours and twenty minutes later we reached the top, to collapse in the Sherpa's house as the mists came back and rain began to fall.

It was the usual house with pictures of the King of Nepal, copper bowls, chickens, staved barrels for chang (rice or barley flour beer).

The house filled as Sherpas and Sherpanis retired from the bad weather. All sat around drinking chang. The house is of stout stone walls, gaps filled with mud, with wooden beams lashed with split bamboo. On this rest the split wooden slates which are held down by rocks. All the interior walls and ceiling are black from soot and tar.

&

John ...

Rained in the night, dripping through the roof on to our bags, and it was still raining in the morning. It stopped by the time we got on the road but it was still very dull. We descended through the maize fields, but then seemed to lose the path in dense shrubbery. The path dropped steeply to the river where we lost Dave, who had stopped off in the bushes. A well-built Swiss bridge crossed the Dudh Kosi River, which was fed by water from Everest. It came as a nasty surprise to find that we were going up steeply once more.

'We looked into the biggest, deepest valley, I had ever seen in my life'

We had dinner in a village built amid jumbled boulders. It was steeply upwards again after dinner and then round to a col where

LP pointed out the track ahead, which zigzagged up the mountainside to a small house on the edge of the clouds. The Dudh Kosi valley was tremendously steep, with huge towering mountains disappearing into the clouds on either flank. The track was not as bad as we had anticipated and Johnny and I caught up with Dave and then went on to the house in quick time. As we moved into the house it came on to rain heavily and I waited outside for Pam. A Sherpa house, so we were sleeping inside again. The atmosphere was fabulous. There were 21 people altogether, with the family, our party and the odd porters. I slept next to the 'chang' brewing barrel, which smelled like rough cider.

Spent the night at the 'Rat House' (near Bupsa), altitude 7,612ft.
6 miles; 3,281ft ascent; 1,706ft descent.

&

74

Memories 2010

David …

As the weather closed in we settled into the Sherpa house to escape the rain, and if ever we were at the heart of the Nepalese tradition of travellers being offered shelter, then this was it. The fire burned and we sat in the near darkness watching the life of the house. More travellers arrived and each group cooked their meal and sat about talking. The family were part of it all without having to contribute to the activity. As the fire died down everyone went early to bed using their very basic blanket-cum-scarf for cover. Our sleeping bags were luxury by comparison.

❧

Les …

Things gradually improved as I got fitter and began to enjoy the experience. I can't say I enjoyed the actual physical effort. It didn't help when LP would point out a ridge in the far distance on the other side of a deep valley as our destination, not for the day but for lunch! I looked forward to the lunch stops and overnight stops when Kaman went on ahead and lit a fire to boil water for endless cups of tea. Then he and LP would make boiled eggs and chapattis or some kind of curry with ever-increasing quantities of rice. In the first few days we started off each evening cooking with half a cup of dried rice per person, but before long as we burned up more and more calories, we were consuming more than a cup each.

Thursday 29ᵗʰ February, Day 11

David …

In all, 21 'guests' arrived last night. I slept alongside two Sherpas – we all have fleas by now. John and Pam are the worst affected. Bed at 6.45pm and up at 5.30am, although we had been disturbed from about 3.00am onwards as the various groups left. They must be able to see in the dark. John, sleeping near the chang barrel, had a scuffle with a rat in the night. Even as we cooked breakfast others arrived to cook theirs, after being on the road for hours.

High peaks all around, though relatively insignificant ones. They are not even named as they are only 20,000ft! We rushed about peering through the holes in the mist at them. Lunch high on a ridge from where we could see a vast panorama with Cho Oyu in the middle, flanked by smaller but beautiful snow peaks. Kangchung to the right, then the ridge hid the ring of higher peaks.

Beautiful primroses grew in the damp, sheltered gullies. On the trail we met a Canadian who was full of admiration for the snows, peaks and valleys. He chatted away, giving us all sorts of bits of news and information. His Sherpa, Pasang, had been on the South Col three times. He also had three real jovial Sherpanis carrying all his gear.

Coming down through the icy forest I slipped and wrenched my knee a bit. The yak pack animals had no trouble, their herdsmen driving them along with whistles and yells. One driver told me how expensive they were – 300 rupees (£10); ordinary cows are cheaper at about 70-80 rupees (£2 to £3). We spent the night at LP's grandfather's.

❧

John …   Had a brush with a rat in the night. It ran over my face – nasty! Some of the sleepers were getting up at 2.00am and the family woke at 4.00am. In fact we were the only ones still in bed when our party woke at daybreak. The cloud broke up and we caught a magnificent view of a peak at close range through a hole in the cloud.

We set off more or less together, upwards again through frosty pine forests. We travelled behind a yak train for a bit before overtaking and catching up Dave and Johnny. We rushed on to the col where we were sure there would be a good view. It becomes increasingly difficult to describe the magnificent views such as this, but again it was breath-taking, and we could see the mighty Cho Oyo and Kangchung. I photographed them and studied them through binoculars. It was great, actually seeing famous 26,000ft mountains.

We had pancakes for lunch at 9.00am and then chatted with an elderly Canadian who was also on a trek.

A steep path, covered with ice and snow, which had to be negotiated very carefully, led to the stream bottom, from whence we traversed the sunny hillside to another col. On the way we stopped on a cultivated terrace at LP's uncle's home to sample some chang. From the col we descended steeply into the inner bowels of this, the biggest, deepest valley I had ever seen in my life. Down and down through the forests with beautiful majestic scenery on all sides.

At LP's father's house, situated on a delightful terrace above the valley bottom, we found that Dave had overshot. Rather than push on to the next village, I ran ahead to catch him up. I followed his footprints and found him well up the mountainside, fortunately waiting. We had another fine meal. LP's father was apparently dead, but we were introduced to his grandfather and grandmother. There was an airstrip on a ledge 1,000ft or so above us.

> Spent the night at LP's grandfather's house (Nangbug near Lukla), 8,530ft.
> 9 miles; 3,805ft ascent; 2,756ft descent.

Memories 2010

We entered LP's grandfather's house by way of steps on the end of the balcony. The yaks were housed downstairs and the family lived in one large room upstairs. The covered veranda formed a walkway from the steps along the front of the house. At the top of the stairs was an elongated slot in the planks that formed the floor. Nearby was a pile of pine needles: this was the family toilet. They squatted over the slot and then brushed fresh pine needles to fall on the pile below. Down in the animal quarters was a pyramid of human excreta and pine needles that would be cleared out when the animal stalls were cleared and the manure spread on the fields.

I didn't use it, of course. I was using so much energy that I didn't have much to spare and as a consequence I needed to go to the toilet only rarely – about six times, I think, in the 27 days. Three or four days after leaving Everest I was called into the rhododendron bushes

Top: Dawn over our house near Bupsa, where John had a 'brush with a rat'.

Above: David and John pause to admire the view

David …

alongside the path. I found myself looking out across the bushes and intermediate mountains into the face of Mount Everest. It was my last view of the mountain!

❧

John ... It was around this point in our trek that LP introduced 'Sherpa potatoes' into our diet. These were potatoes boiled in their skins and then peeled while still hot, using a thumbnail. Then they were put back in the pan and mixed with ghee. We found them delicious and gave not a thought to the lack of hygiene. Also we delighted in 'chilli tomatoes' which were tomatoes baked and mixed with chilli powder.

Friday 1st March, Day 12

David ... LP did not return until breakfast. Kaman saw to breakfast in his absence. When he did return he was obviously under the weather from too much drink. All day he was a drag on our hope to get to Namche. He was slow and lethargic, stopping for rests and generally determined to stop as soon as possible. Kaman seemed worried and embarrassed by LP's behaviour.

While waiting for porridge, we sat staring at the golden tips of mountains that were just clear of the mists. I was glad to get up, though still tired after a disturbed night because two babies, sleeping near, cried at regular intervals.

We had an easy three-hour stroll, covering the ground I had already done yesterday in my super-fit burst at the front. John had to chase after me and bring me back. It was easy because we were forever waiting for our Sherpa. He was under the influence of the yak drivers, who were having a leisurely time strolling home, calling in at all the chang stops. Another Sherpa who we nicknamed 'Joe Brown' took over from LP to cook our dinner.

One hour downhill, then a long wait for LP who had been at the hooch again. During the day it was a steady ascent to the col where we had lunch. Below was a fantastic valley with sheer walls cut by centuries of rushing water. By the trail we met five Americans who had flown in to Lukla and were on their way to fly out again. They had taken eight days to reach Base Camp from Namche. Up there they had good weather with low temperatures. One woman had a flower in her hair; in answer to our question she said it was the first flower she had seen up here so she picked it! Flying out may be easy, but the beauties and interests of Nepal are lost to those who arrive that way. Also, arriving by air will dump them completely unfit high in the Himalaya. I prefer our way.

All afternoon, in between halts for LP, we wandered up the Dudh Kosi. The path clung tightly to the river bank and the green glacier water spilled over the boulders. For two hours we really scorched along the pine-covered paths, scuffing the pine needles with our tiring feet. We scorched because we were bored by the slow pace determined by LP.

We stayed at a Sherpa house about two hours from Namche, a large house, well stocked. The friendly Sherpa showed us many of his religious relics that are so valuable to him. Similar ones are for sale in Kathmandu for many hundreds of rupees. One long narrow book of prayers supposedly protected the carrier from bullets or knife thrusts.

In the Sherpa – Buddhist – areas, chortens and mani walls (structures that protect from bad and evil spirits) are very common along the paths. The walls of prayer stones and boulders, carved centuries ago with religious inscriptions, split the paths: uphill traffic to the left, downhill to the right. Every summit on the path has prayer flags and prayer stones.

෨

St David's Day. LP was out for the night. Early in the morning I joined Kaman by the fire to make coffee, while in the dim light everyone else still slumbered. We set off along the same path as Dave and I had trodden the night before. It was easy going for some time along a gentle uphill rise. LP lagged a long way behind and at dinner time, after waiting for nearly an hour, we found him drunk.

The afternoon's walk was very pleasant up the gently rising river bed, passing pine forests, gushing torrents and steep rock walls. It was marred though by having to wait yet another 45 minutes for a drunken LP. We told him off when he arrived and he followed us up the valley at a good pace. We met several Americans who had flown in to Lukla.

John ...

Stopped for the night in a house at the bottom of the hill to Namche. It was another house of basic Sherpa design, owned by a young couple. Johnny gave LP a dressing down and after that he improved, even refusing more drink.

Spent the night at Benkar, Altitude 8,923ft.

6 miles; 1,181ft ascent; 1,050ft descent

❧

Johnny ...

The morning routine begins early in Nepal. Long before dawn people are on the move. We rose early and after a hasty breakfast of tea and heavily sugared porridge we were walking again, dreading the moment that the sweltering sun would mount the ridge and crawl up to bathe us in sweat once more. Day after day this routine is continued, mile after mile, ridge after ridge, valley after valley, you walk.

'We caught our first view of Mount Everest'

A note of the physical aspect of the country we cross: the three main features of the route to Namche Bazaar are the huge ridges. These

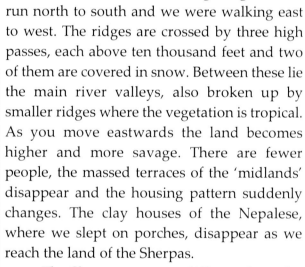

run north to south and we were walking east to west. The ridges are crossed by three high passes, each above ten thousand feet and two of them are covered in snow. Between these lie the main river valleys, also broken up by smaller ridges where the vegetation is tropical. As you move eastwards the land becomes higher and more savage. There are fewer people, the massed terraces of the 'midlands' disappear and the housing pattern suddenly changes. The clay houses of the Nepalese, where we slept on porches, disappear as we reach the land of the Sherpas.

The Sherpas are very different from the Nepalese farmers. They are stocky, talkative and infinitely more sophisticated, although still in the Middle Ages in terms of their way of life. They are wealthier, living in wooden or stone houses and are herders. Their houses are all the same style, with one room that is used for everything – cooking, sleeping and toilet. All life goes on in this room. The bed, fire, a low bench that serves as table, storage jars and great brass pitchers for water and corn are all in the same places in every house. No house has a chimney and when the fire is going full blast the room is thick with wood smoke. We found this almost unbearable but the Sherpas seemed not to mind at all.

We stayed in these houses for most of the trek, at a cost of just two rupees a night – about a quarter of a penny. This was 'daura' or wood money, to pay for the wood we used to prepare our meals. Water was free and Kaman often went out with the water barrel to refill the pitcher. Everything else we used was given freely and apart from luxuries such as sugar and salt, commodities were fairly cheap.

Occasionally our Sherpa would get hold of some buffalo meat or a cock chicken – one cost us only 6s 0d and was big enough to feed all of us. In Namche we ate yak meat; killing yaks is banned in Nepal but the Sherpas pay little attention to such laws. Potatoes cooked in every possible way form the basis of their diet, and eggs and milk provide their major protein balance.

Memories 2010

We were so focused on our march and our objective that it was a real nuisance when LP arrived drunk. He had been so good in the earlier days and we felt comfortable in his care. We couldn't lose our pace and focus by allowing him to slow the pace to a rest day. I was incredibly frustrated and found it difficult. The other Sherpas must have known that and readily covered for him. A complete stranger took on his duties: out of loyalty to the Sherpa tradition, or out of respect for travellers?

David ...

જી

When we arrived in Sherpa country we slept inside the houses. When darkness fell the only light came from the fire or its embers. We took a few candles, but our hosts didn't have them and so we hardly used them. The Sherpas managed with the ambient light from the fire, which shone from small reflective pieces of rock

John ...

embedded in the shelves and posts, or sometimes dabs of paint. When they needed stronger light they used what they proudly declared were 'Sherpa candles'. These were thin shavings of wood placed on top of the earthen fireplaces and set on fire. They gave an intense bright light for around 30 seconds, enabling them to perform a more intricate task – as long as they did it quickly!

Saturday 2nd March, Day 13

David …   After a good night's sleep we left for Namche Bazaar. In the house the wife, husband and the three children were all in the one bed near the fire. Before we left we tried Tibetan Tea. It is made as follows: boil tea; add Ghee (purified butter) and salt into the long wooden tube; pour in the tea and plunge the mixture with the wooden stick until all is thoroughly mixed; re-boil and drink. The result is a very rich, salty tea which I didn't like. Pam said she enjoyed it.

Easy walk to the bottom of Namche Hill, amid scenery of pines, snows and ice falls which hang like green or blue chandeliers. Many porters were on the move, heading for Namche market. Namche sits in a hanging valley on the top of a very steep hill, which took us about one and a half hours to ascend. Half way up at a small resting place, we caught our first glimpse of Everest. The many closer peaks made the tiny rock triangle of Everest seem rather unimpressive. It is hard to write of the full majesty of the scenery and tiredness each night makes these notes just a quick, scribbled memo.

Namche Bazaar is a fabulous place of grey stone houses clustered in the bowl of a hanging valley, beneath a big black peak. I imagine the mining village at the base of Snowdon at Llyn Llydaw or Glaslyn would have had this atmosphere. Opposite where we are staying is a vast ice gulley. We are in the best Sherpa house yet, materially. The owner is the man who has been bringing the yaks along for the last two days. He and his father have been on many expeditions. On a recent successful Indian expedition, one of his sons was the Assistant Sirdar (the Sirdar is the lead Sherpa and manages them on an expedition). There was much mountaineering equipment lying about the house.

The first person we met was a New Zealand doctor who runs a

hospital up at Khunde. Standing in the market amid the hill-men, we had a long, very informative chat with him. The hospital is financed by the New Zealand Sherpa Trust Fund founded by Edmund Hillary. All the monies come from mountaineers and donations from the general public. Lots of general chat about the area, also about Peter Mulgrew's *'No Place for Men'* ((Mulgrew was a New Zealand mountaineer)). As we were nattering LP came to tell us that the local Civil Officer wanted to see us. He is the civilian governor of the district. It was quite a worthless visit because he had nothing to say and we all sat in an awkward silence.

Shopped in the market which was full of Tibetan types. We spent late afternoon preparing our supplies for Base Camp. It is cold here at 11,000ft.

Les has decided to stay here in Namche; he can't face the walk. Kaman suffers bad headaches at this altitude so he will stay and look after Les, on half pay. We hired a new porter, Na Temba, for high altitude work. He gets eight rupees plus food.

Fantastic evening meal of Horlicks meals and Sherpa potatoes.

Above Left:
'Namche Bazar is a fabulous place of grey stone houses clustered in the bowl of a hanging valley'.

Above Right:
Namche is fantastic, no roads,, thin air and surrounded by huge spectacular peaks'.

Dr John McKinnon the New Zealand doctor and his family at Khunde

LP, drunk again, appeared later with a bowl of curried yak meat. This was after we had said we didn't want any because the Horlicks meals were filling. In his drunken babblings he insisted on giving us the food as a present, partly as a peace offering for drinking again. Again other Sherpas and Kaman filled in for him by doing the chores.

ɕ

John ... After about 3.00am or 4.00am I didn't sleep too well; as soon as I saw the fire flickering I was in the habit of getting up. I joined Kaman again by the fire. After we set off we soon reached the steep hill to Namche and, with the others ahead, Pam and I began to plod up it. About half way up Les, Johnny and LP had stopped and we caught our first view of Mount Everest: it didn't look as impressive as we had imagined, but it was wonderful to gaze and think that it was the highest mountain in the world.

Half an hour further on we rounded a corner to see the long-awaited Namche Bazaar situated high up in a little hanging valley. Our house in Namche was the best we had yet stayed at. It had glass windows, bits of carpet and a rudimentary chimney. We checked in at the police post and then returned for a pancake dinner. Afterwards we went shopping at the thriving Saturday market. Here we met the local New Zealand doctor and had an informative and interesting talk.

He promised to lend us his map; Johnny and I could pick it up next day.

Spent the afternoon preparing soup and writing this log. Hope to prepare for the 'final push' up to Base Camp later on. LP suggested we hire a high altitude porter and when we agreed he produced one, magician-like, from the other room. He was called Na Temba.

Made a delicious evening meal of Horlicks dehydrated meals, Sherpa spuds and yak meat. The latter was brought by LP (drunk again) as a peace offering. He was severely reprimanded. The atmosphere here in Namche is fantastic – a world of its own with no roads or communication with the outside world, thin air, and surrounded by huge spectacular peaks. In the backstreets, though, life was much the same as anywhere else.

Spent the night in Namche Bazaar, altitude 11,289ft.

5 miles; 2,625ft ascent; 262ft descent.

Memories 2010

I don't remember how we came to be in the house of the local school master but he was a really friendly guy. He had books. He could read. He was busy teaching his young nephew to read and speak English. He sat on the bed with the boy cuddled close and they read and talked and practised words in English. Around them the big pot-bellied brass water bowls gleamed in the firelight. One of the shutters was open and light fell across the finger-painted white paint splodges that marked the fronts of the shelves, every surface and the window frames.

Downstairs the yaks coughed and chaffed at their rope bindings. As I stepped out of the house and stood on the steep bank that was a kind of garden, the lady of the house in full Sherpa thick black skirt and multi-coloured apron squatted down at my side and urinated. The yellow liquid ran out from under her raised skirts and under my boots as I gazed at the ice gully across the valley and the market just below.

David …

'…it can't be healthy to live in darkness filled with smoke'

John ...   Kaman bought a small rug in the market to take back to Kathmandu, using some of the wages we had paid him. He seemed so pleased with his acquisition that I was very touched by his offer to let me, or Pam, sleep on it. My already immense respect for this humble and honest man grew enormously. I have told this story to children in school assemblies a number of times over the years as an example of human goodness. I suppose we were very lucky that LP chose such a man to be our porter.

Les decided to stay and rest in Namche Bazaar and await our return in five days. My sleeping bag wasn't as good as Les's and he offered to swap. I was very touched by his generosity. It might not have been on a par with Captain Oates walking out into the blizzard, but when you consider how infested we were with fleas and how little we were able to wash, the gesture was above and beyond the call of duty. I jumped at the offer and it was a great help to me. I somehow felt his fleas would be cleaner than mine!

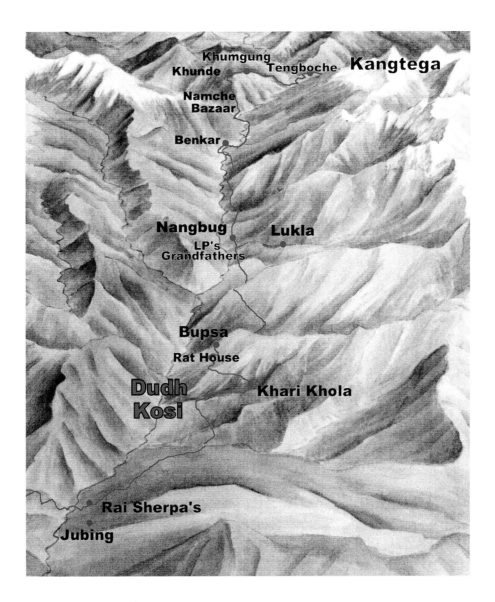

A painting by Andy Birkby showing the route up the Namche Valley.

The last leg to Kala Pattar at the foot of Mount Everest, at an altitude of 18,200ft.

The British Mountaineering Council now recommend that above 3000m (9842ft), trekkers should sleep no more than 300m (984ft) higher each day and have a day's rest every three days. By this formula the walk from Namche Bazaar to Lobuche should take six days. In our innocence we took two days.

Chapter 7

To the Foot of the Mighty Everest

Sunday 3rd March, Day 14

Early to rise so we could be away; finally trudged off at 7.45am in bright sunshine. The surrounding peaks looked enormous against the blue sky. A cwm (bowl-shaped valley) behind Namche was blindingly bright.

David ...

Once over the first rise above Namche Bazaar, Everest was clearly visible over the Nuptse Ridge. To the right and left of it snow peaks craned their necks to peep at the path we were to follow; a long contouring path that had to plunge down to the river before climbing again to Tengboche. Most impressive of all was Ama Dablam, sheer, impregnable, disdainful, her battlements rising straight up from the river's bank. We were walking rather slowly from the compelling sights that forced us to walk more slowly than usual. From above the dark roaring depths, the track led down through the woods to the river.

From the green, swiftly flowing river the route went slowly up through rhododendron woods ringing with the sound of axes. Above the woods the gradient became more gentle. Going up to the monastery at 14,000ft, I found the first real effects of altitude start to tell.

John and Johnny caught us up at Tengboche after detouring to Khunde to borrow the map offered by the New Zealand doctor. From the small plateau where the exquisite monastery sits the scenery was unbelievable and the scale beyond comprehension. Ama Dablam is

Right: Ama Dablam from the Hospital.

Below: The peaks behind Namche from Tengboche.

Left: 'Most impressive of all was Ama Dablam, sheer, impregnable, disdainful ...'

Left: The surrounding peaks looked enormous against the blue sky'.

always demanding to be photographed, like a mannequin. Everest hid behind the finest shawl of wind-blown chiffon.

Pangboche was just one and a half hours up the valley. We stayed the night there, in the centre of the spartan village. Stark greys and browns of the small fields in this early spring are still being bitten by late frosts. Our hostess is a wrinkled, dirty woman. She has two small children who must be her own as no one else appeared. At bedtime, 7.30pm, she rolled herself and the two mites into a bundle of rags near the fire.

Na Temba developed an awful blister but he did not stop. All around the primitive dwellings are mountains, mountains and mountains.

ço

We rose early and quickly got organised. Johnny and I left for Khunde to pick up the map that the New Zealand doctor had offered to lend. We gained ground quickly but were feeling the altitude. En route we passed an English chap who was in the army in Singapore. We also met the Swiss couple's Sherpa – they were staying at Khumjung, having had a rest day in Junbesi. We lost the track at one point but eventually found the right track up to the hospital. After living in Sherpa houses, it was fantastic to see a well-organised, clean painted room with all the neatly laid-out shelves. We were shown round and then chatted with the doctor and his wife over coffee and biscuits.

John ...

We left for Tengboche, which involved a descent and steep ascent. We covered it in quick time despite still feeling the altitude a little. We met the others who had not long arrived. All day we had magnificent views of Ama Dablam, a thoroughly impregnable-looking peak. Everest was beginning to look bigger as it peeped over the steep precipices of Nuptse. At dinner we tried some very tasty Sherpa biscuits.

There was a short walk down snow-covered slopes. Na Temba showed us he had a huge blister. We crossed the raging stream and walked up the other side to Pangboche. Na Temba seemed a good bloke, but was having difficulty on the snow, and LP seemed a little subdued.

91

We were now only two days from the great turning point of the expedition, for then we would be on the Khumbu Glacier and facing westwards, and home, after 150 foot-miles and 9,000 car-miles. What a distance! I must have got used to it as I didn't feel I was particularly far from home. What a fantastic land this is! The whole purpose of a Sherpa family's life is to feed itself and survive. To that end the whole of their lives is spent in labour. An old woman and two kids live in the house in Pangboche where we stayed the night.

Spent the night in Pangboche, altitude 12,861ft.

8 miles; 3,937ft ascent; 2,231ft descent.

~

Johnny ... In Khunde, at 12,000ft, we visited the hospital built by Sir Edmund Hillary and met the doctor from New Zealand, John McKinnon. He told us much about these mountain people and their health problems. Most of the hospital is given over to TB patients, for this is the most virulent disease among the Sherpas. Goitres and thyroid problems are the other major diseases as the water they drink contains no iodine. McKinnon is a fantastic person, performing most duties of a general practitioner as well as dentist, midwife and general adviser. His wife, equally dedicated, teaches at the nearby Hillary School in Khumjung.

Memories 2010

Les ... Having struggled to Namche I decided I had had enough walking. I made arrangements to stay there in the house with the local schoolteacher and his family. By that time I had seen most of the big peaks and I welcomed the opportunity to relax and soak up the local atmosphere, take some photos, do some sketching and explore the area.

With the others gone, Kaman, being a lowlander and ill-equipped for altitude, stayed with me. He prepared my meals, washed up and generally looked after me. He was on reduced wages because he wasn't carrying, and for this and a few packets of incredibly cheap cigarettes bought in the local shop, he acted almost as my personal servant.

I went to visit the local school. By our standards, it was bedlam. The two oldest pupils were learning English, yelling at the tops of their voices "Ram is sitting. Gita is standing," over and over again. They were following a text book while banging their desks in time to the chant.

One evening I was invited to a 'party' by the schoolteacher but when I got there – a communal room with seats around the edge like a school dance – I discovered that everyone was expected to make a contribution. Not having much cash and aware of our precarious financial position, I made an excuse and left.

The rest of the time I spent wandering about to such an extent that I attracted the attention of the officer in charge of the small garrison of police in the village. He came out to quiz me when I was walking around the outskirts of the village. He was very pleasant and polite and complimented me on my drawings before establishing my identity, where I was from and what I was doing, and then leaving me to carry on.

Letter home from Les

A mother and child outside our house taken by Les ...' I am amusing myself by wandering round and taking photographs'.

Namche Bazaar, Nepal, 3rd March 1968

Dear All,

After an exhausting 12 days' march we have finally arrived in Namche Bazaar, an important market village about 20 miles from Mount Everest. We hired a Sherpa in Kathmandu and also a Nepalese porter to carry our gear and food etc – the Sherpa for 10 rupees a day (6s 8d) and the Nepalese for eight rupees a day. We supply the Sherpa with food but the Nepalese buys his own. The Sherpa carries 40lb of equipment but also acts as guide and interpreter (although his English isn't all that good), which explains why he is paid more. Also the Sherpas consider themselves superior to other Nepalese and so justify a higher salary.

Kaman washing up during the five days at Namche with Les.

In fact the Nepalese is a much nicer fellow, as we have discovered since we set off, although he doesn't speak a word of English. He carries 80lb without complaining. It may not sound much but when you consider that the road (the main road from Kathmandu to Eastern Nepal, which in places hardly warrants the description of path) climbs and falls steeply over its whole length like a succession of staircases, and that he carries this weight in a basket on his back held in place only by a woven strap over his head (no shoulder straps), and moreover, that he walks in bare feet, it is quite an achievement.

The first 30 miles of the 150-mile journey to Namche is served by a good road and a frightening bus journey, of which we took advantage. The first few days walking after that were sheer purgatory, especially for me, not being as fit as the other athletic types and I didn't think I was going to last out the journey. But after a while the blisters healed and the stiffness wore off and it wasn't too bad.

The Sherpa, who says his name is 'LP' when written in English, really came into his own during the first part of the journey. He would wake us in the morning with a cup of tea and then make breakfast of porridge. At lunch he has provided us with a curry or omelettes or pancakes and in the evening with more curry. He's also been able to buy rice, sugar and other necessities at the local prices and not the tourist prices we usually have to pay. He also does the washing up and washes our socks etc. It's a bit like having a valet. However, since he got nearer home (near Namche) he's been meeting some of his friends and getting drunk fairly regularly, so we've stopped his pay until we get back to Kathmandu.

We have brought a mountain tent with us for use higher up but all along the way we have been staying in local houses; sleeping on the verandas of Nepalese houses (the lowland ones where it is warmer) and inside Sherpa houses. In the Nepalese houses we had to fight for sleeping room with dogs, chickens, goats, rats and mice, and in the

Sherpa houses just with rats and people. We are all thoroughly flea-ridden at the moment.

The absolute primitiveness of life here is amazing. To start with, there are no roads, no electricity, no piped water, no sanitation and no shops except in the larger villages like Namche (population about 200, fifty per cent of whom are civil administrators, Nepalese army and police and Indian Army personnel). Because all commodities not locally produced have to be brought in on porters' backs it makes everything very expensive, therefore most households are self-sufficient, living off the land.

The Nepalese houses are one-roomed affairs with a poorly-thatched veranda. In the middle of the house is a fireplace with a fire, burning eternally. They don't go in for windows or chimneys so the atmosphere is unbearable, which is why we sleep outside. The houses are stone built and there is plenty of stone around so it is difficult to understand why they don't construct outbuildings; perhaps because they haven't the tools to make the wooden joists and the like. Most of the timber is not sawn or planed but split with axes and wedges. So, with only the one room of the house available for all uses, at night the animals – chickens, dogs, rats, sheep and cattle etc – are driven into the house to sleep with the extended family, contributing to the fug inside.

The Sherpa houses are generally bigger and usually have two-storeys. The animals sleep below and the people live upstairs. They keep different animals from the lowland Nepalese, the most common being the most peculiar animal we have yet come across, the half-yak. This is a cross between a cow and a yak and is used for milk and as a beast of burden. It is also eaten on the sly by the Sherpas, who are Buddhist and therefore don't consider the animal sacred, as the Hindus do. But because most of the administration is Hindu they face penalties if they are caught.

Because of the climate the houses are much more solidly built than the Nepalese ones and some even have glass in the windows. But in both types when darkness falls the only light is from the fire or tapers made from split bamboo, or on very rare occasions, an oil lamp. How they manage to see after dark is beyond me. The Sherpas appear far more prosperous than the average Nepalese and their houses are crammed with possessions – bowls by the dozen made from copper and brass, cooking instruments, occasional transistor radios and piles of clothing left behind by all the various expeditions there have been in this area.

I am staying at the moment in the best house we have yet seen. It even has two rooms upstairs, which is unusual. The other four of our party have set off up the valley to Everest Base Camp and the Khumbu Glacier. After 12 days' walking I couldn't face it, so I've stayed here to wander around and take photos, something I didn't have the mental energy to do when we were walking.

The Nepalese porter, whose name is Kaman, has also stayed behind because he is a lowlander; he hasn't any shoes anyway for the snow and ice. He is virtually my personal servant but because he isn't carrying anything he is on half pay (2s 8d per day). He is doing all my cooking and washing etc, and has just made me some coffee at 9.30am. Our stock of candles is dwindling fast, but we have been so exhausted with walking that we have been going to bed just after dark at about 7.00pm and getting up at dawn at about 6.00am, getting eleven solid hours' sleep.

The others should be away for about five days. Tomorrow I am going up the valley to the next village where there is a small hospital run by two New Zealanders. I shall not have missed much except a few more days' walking and a couple of cold nights spent on a glacier (it's cold enough here at night). All the major peaks in the area can be seen from the immediate vicinity of Namche.

It's eight days' walk back from here to Kathmandu. We are all now indescribably filthy and we are looking forward to the comparative civilisation and comfort of the Camp Hotel. I shan't be able to post this until we get back but I thought I might as well make good use of my time here. I will write again from Kathmandu.

Love Les

PS. Paper's got a bit grotty because it has been chucking around in my rucksack for a month.

Monday 4th March, Day 15

I had a poor night's sleep due to the altitude and was awake for a long time with a severe headache. At 6.00am we saw the most amazing panorama. Clouds hurried up and down the gulleys. Everest was hidden completely. Ama Dablam put on a new gown and cast a perfect replica of itself on to the clouds. Snow had fallen in the valley, giving a thin veil to the bitter soil; mountains frolicked in and out of the mist. The shark's-fin peak of Kangtega was the first to find the morning light. Tramserku Ridge gleamed like a silver coxcomb. All the others were just magnificent. Bought some firewood to take with us; LP and Na Temba are carrying it.

Pheriche was our lunch destination, a collection of stone huts 600ft to 700ft higher than our starting point. The village was an amazing collection of dry-stone-walled shacks, each enclosed in a maze of dry-stone walls. They are built from stones that were lying about on the surface and are completely camouflaged against the river valley. We cooked a meal in the only hut that was occupied. A young lad, clad in raw sheepskin, was looking after yaks belonging to the monastery. As we ate, one or two hardy characters called in as they passed.

Once on the moraine, we slowed down, picking our way carefully over the loose rubble, gaining altitude all the time. All traces of Pheriche disappeared as the cloud filled the valley and cold flurries of snow began to fall. We had to collect firewood from the last bits of scrub – there is none higher up. Heavy snow and wind bustled us up the valley and along the moraine up to the solitary hut at Lobuche,

Above Left:
Morning frost
outside our house
in Pangboche,
looking back
towards Namche

Above Right:
Packing our bags
at Pheriche as
clouds begin to fill
the valley.

David …

Our nylon suits proved their worth in the wind and snow.

Lobuche is an old stone Yak House set high in the snows right below the 'Mother of the Gods' (Chomolungma, the Tibetan name for Mount Everest was translated as meaning 'Goddess Mother of the World'). LP was quickly into action to make a brew. The six of us only just fit in the house, among old fireplaces and piles of ash. So near to our goal, but snow is still falling heavily and LP has prepared us for disappointment by warning us that four or five feet might fall overnight, with the possibility of being snowed in.

I love the mountains in snow, with their huddled silence, but I hope that it stops to allow us to move up tomorrow. There's so much to remember: the snow-covered glacier, loose moraine, carrying firewood, huddled in warm clothing, signs of others using the hut over many

Near Pheriche - John reading the map lent to us by Dr John Mckinnon.

years, ice on my beard, fresh tingling cheeks. I love the snow and the crystal, clear-cut atmosphere.

John ...

We left Pangboche and made good time up the river valley, with good views again of Ama Dablam, but menacing cloud around Mount Everest. The cloud grew thicker and by the time we reached Pheriche the sky was completely overcast. We had dinner in a straw-filled barn with a young chap clothed completely in sheepskin. We had taken wood from Pangboche, but hoped to collect more en route.

Pheriche was particularly uninhabited, just odd little stone huts with walls marking fields. As we ascended at the end of the valley we began to feel the altitude again. Then it began to snow, making the prospect most miserable. We had a short rest in the barn at Duglha

The huge pyramid of Pumori lay ahead of us ... Fresh snow made the path quite difficult over the loose moraine'.

and then climbed the moraine, pausing periodically to collect wood.

It snowed more heavily and as we traversed the top of the moraine it was like a winter's day in the Cairngorms. We fought on in our waterproofs, what a change from the preceding days. The barn at Lobuche was reminiscent of the Etchechan Bothy in the Cairngorms, except that this one had a hole in the roof that Dave mended. It was tremendously smoky and we occasionally had to go out into the snow for a breath of fresh air. Eventually we got used to it.

When I went out for my late night final it was still snowing, but I could see the moon shining through. Dave had left the matches at Pangboche and we only had three left. So we had to hope like hell for a good day on the morrow, and then we could make a quick dash to Base Camp and back. We could possibly have waited one day by keeping the fire in all day.

Spent the night at Lobuche, altitude 16,175ft.

8.5 miles; 3,281ft ascent; 164ft descent.

Memories 2010

As we neared Everest the altitude really began to tell. I had no experience of altitude and didn't know what to expect. My head

David ...

At Pheriche, 'we had dinner in a straw filled barn with a young chap clothed completely in sheepskin'.

ached constantly and breathing, gasping, did not draw in enough oxygen for comfort. My knowledge of acclimatisation was nil and I presumed our trek would have helped us. I felt bad in my head and was really glad to rest at Pheriche. It was an incredibly atmospheric place with its dry-stone walls and sense of complete isolation.

The young lad in his sheepskin suit stank of roughly cured skin. It was one of those smells that transported us back through history – cave men stank like that. In the Middle Ages and later, people stank of the bacon sewn into their clothes to ward off the plague or other illnesses. It wasn't just that they didn't wash that they were very smelly. The very skins they were wearing in those days were stomach turning. Remember Afghan jackets? They were sweet by comparison. And it must have been a really powerful smell because we were pretty rank ourselves! I am not sure I had many fleas because I filled my bag with DDT powder after a scabby dog in Fatehpur Sikri took a liking to sleeping on my bed. I remember thinking that it cured the fleas but was none too healthy to sleep in!

As we moved up I was a little worried by our collection of firewood. At that altitude it would be slow growing and difficult to replace the wood that we used. We pulled up whatever we could and piled it on our sacks. I'll bet there is none there now. When we arrived at Lobuche we had firewood but I have absolutely no recollection of having only three matches. Needless to say, if it was my fault, I did not record it in my diary.

John ... Dave was so reliable as an organiser and had bailed me out on countless occasions when we were camping at home. It was almost like relying on Mum and Dad when I was little. But he forgot the matches! We found three in his rucksack so we could, with care, light a fire. I was annoyed at first but realised that without Dave's organisational skills and self-discipline we would probably not have got to Kathmandu, let alone within a day's walk from Everest. It was good in a way to realise he was only human like the rest of us.

'We were surrounded by peaks of such grandeur that no sight can be more imposing even if I live to be ninety...'

Tuesday 5ᵗʰ March, Day 16

David ...

After all the horror of yesterday's snow, low cloud and the threat of being snowed in, today dawned brilliantly clear. Probably my best day ever, weather-wise. I had a poor night's sleep because of the thin atmosphere. Any movement in sleep brought me back to consciousness, gasping for air. It was bitterly cold and I had a bad headache. Rats ate all our boiled sweets and nibbled our cocoa and porridge. We changed our plans from a bivouac at Gorak Shep to making a quick sortie up there and returning to Lobuche. It was going to be a long day.

Outside, the mighty mountains took on the shades of sunrise. Everything was so clear, each detail of the peaks. Fresh snow made the path quite difficult over the loose moraine. LP had a bad headache and he looked bad, with swollen, sad eyes. The sun was too hot through the thin air. Creeping up the sides of the glacier, beneath the sheer wall of Nuptse on one side and an unnamed peak on the other, we reached Gorak Shep after two and a half hours. There the valley opened slightly where two glaciers meet. Gorak Shep was a clear brown slope alongside the Khumbu Glacier, which we could see pouring out of the Western Cwm.

Above: LP at Gorak Shep ... 'he had a very bad headache but his pride dictated that he must come'.

Right: David on the summit of Kala Pattar March 5th 1968. 'I was standing at the foot of Everest and not many could say that'.

Above Right: John on Kala Pattar ... 'We felt thoroughly exhausted but nonetheless sat there spellbound'.

Above: The view back down the Khumbu Glacier from the top of Kala Pattar.

Left: 'The return to Lobuche was the longest four hours I have known'.

Left: Pumori from the summit of Kala Pattar.

The view of Mount Everest unfolds as we climb above Gorak Shep.

At the foot of Gorak Shep we left LP with all our gear as we thrust up Kala Pattar hill, at 18,200ft. John was feeling bad with altitude sickness; Pam was pretty exhausted. Johnny tired rapidly, until I was left the fittest. It took one and quarter hours to climb the 1,000ft. Johnny was for giving up but I pushed him to make the top. From the summit of the ridge running up to Pumori the views were tremendous: Everest, Ama Dablam, Pumori and 10,000 others. Every mountain so clear, no haze, no mist or cloud. Just clear bright sunshine.

Coming down was great, even though I was tired. Johnny was pale and drawn before we reached Lobuche, but he quickly recovered. John was quite ill and he lay dozing in the tent all evening. But we had done it, Everest Base Camp! (The original Base camp for Mount Everest was around Gorak Shep where you can just see the tip of its summit. However it's not possible to see it from the location of present base camps which are at the foot of the Khumbu Ice Fall. So trekkers usually climb Kala Pattar where there are good views. However, they still rather inaccurately talk about going to Base Camp).

It was a terrific thrill to gaze at the majesty of the world's highest peak. As we watched, the mountains demonstrated their power as an avalanche cascaded down a gulley on Nuptse. We could see the South Col with the snow plume lazily streaming from 29,000ft off the summit of Everest. We were still 11,000ft from the top.

Back at Lobuche we drank cup after cup of tea to satisfy our enormous thirst. On returning we found some new residents, an English Major, serving with the Gurkhas in the Far East, and the Swiss couple that we met many times coming out.

ဆ

John ... The big day dawned absolutely crystal clear. LP had a very bad headache and was slumped in a corner, covered in sleeping bags.

We arranged for Na Temba to come instead but at the last minute LP's pride dictated that he must come. The mountain views were terrific, particularly of Pumori, and we wondered whether it would hold out long enough to get views from Kala Pattar. As we trudged up the snow-covered moraine I began to feel the altitude. After two hours we reached Gorak Shep and above it rose the hill of Kala Pattar. We told LP to wait with the rucksacks while we climbed it. At this point we could just see Mount Everest.

Above the resting place the slope rose steeply and I knew that it was not going to be an easy task. For the next hour and a half Pam and I laboured up the slope – ten steps and then we would flop exhausted on the ground. I have never put so much effort into uphill movement in my life. Twice Pam said she wanted to give up but I knew that for her, like me, it was out of the question. As we scrambled over the summit rocks we could see Johnny, but when we got there all was silent and deserted. Tracks led off down the other side. Dave had Pam's camera and I shouted to him, but there was no reply. Pam was disappointed but I shot off my film in all directions – marvellous views of Everest and my ambition fully realised.

We felt thoroughly exhausted but nonetheless sat there spellbound. All around were huge glistening, spectacular peaks and above them loomed the gigantic form of Everest, on which we could see all the features that we had read so much about. We descended quite quickly but felt absolutely exhausted at Gorak Shep, where we found everyone had gone. Dave returned, fortunately with our duvets.

It must have been the effect of altitude on our brains but everything seemed confused and jumbled up. When Pam and I returned to where we had left our rucksacks they were not there. This was good because we didn't have to carry them, but it was cold and we needed our duvets. I struggled back to camp feeling very ill. Pam stayed with me as I had to rest every five minutes. When I got back to Lobuche I just slumped in the tent and dozed in between being fed.

Spent the night at Lobuche, altitude 16,175ft.

7 miles; 2,018ft ascent; 2,018ft descent. Climbed Kala Pattar at altitude 18,192ft.

෴

Johnny ... No one lives above the village of Pheriche. There was once a settlement as high as Lobuche, at 16,000ft, but now all that remains are the ruins of two or three stone huts. These are used as shelters by trekkers and we spent two nights in one of them. Headaches are a constant reminder that you are living at a point higher than the summit of Mont Blanc.

We walked slowly up the snow-covered moraine of the Khumbu Glacier and at last to Gorak Shep and Base Camp. We were surrounded by huge peaks of such grandeur that it would need much greater ability than mine to describe them. Suffice it to say that I will see no more imposing sight even if I live to be 90. The huge pyramid of Pumori lay ahead of us and ridges connected her to Lobuche to the west and the mass of Everest to the east. The Chinese frontier lies only about a mile away over the Lho Lha Pass. It is so precipitous that frontier guards are not necessary here.

We climbed painfully to the height of 18,200ft on Kala Pattar, a ridge of Pumori, and from there the view cross to Everest was one of awe-inspiring beauty. Its size is beyond belief and it towers above its neighbours like a God. A snow plume, miles long, drifted lazily from its summit. It is easy to see why great men have fought and died to reach its summit.

Altitude threatened. I spent too long looking at this wonder of nature. My head was reeling and my legs were like jelly. I found it extremely hard to get my breath and as I descended the feeling of nausea almost overcame me. The return to Lobuche was the longest four hours I have known, but after a cup of tea and a bowl of soup I recovered and was untroubled again. John felt worse than me and was almost incapable of walking the following day. Pam was very badly blistered by the sun and we all found it almost impossible to sleep.

Memories 2010

David ... The altitude was very debilitating. I breathed hard. I fell asleep quickly but woke up with terrible headaches that drained my body of energy and sapped my willpower. It was not much easier when we began to walk up to and then to climb Kala Pattar. I was so determined to climb that hill to 18,000ft. I struggled and puffed my way, ten paces at a time. I nagged at Johnny to rest and then to move. I counted the steps and bowed my head. I knew I would do it, would have to do it. I held Johnny at one point and pulled him forward.

At the top, when I had got my breath back, I was a mess of emotions. I did shout – one of my whoops – and hailed the mighty Everest. I thought, for once, of my time in hospital and my disability. I felt I had overcome it. It had prevented me joining the RAF – an early teenage fantasy that I feel I would have made a reality. It had prevented me playing sport at grammar school and achieving other things.

But I was standing at the foot of Everest and not many could say that. I wanted to shout and tell people that I had done it. Miss Pearson, the surgeon who had cared for me in Pinderfields and had worked wonders. Mr Roach, the headmaster of Barnsley Grammar School, who had made sure that I was cared for when I returned after my stay in hospital. My mum and dad for their devoted love and care, supporting me so that I could achieve some of my ambitions.

Everest is a highlight of my life because it was such an effort to get there. We did it alone and it required an enormous effort, and that has helped me in many ways. When I have had any doubts I have drawn on the perseverance and determination I knew had got me to Base Camp.

When we arrived in a house or village during the trek I was always exhausted and so thirsty that the first and second cups of tea were truly wonderful. I took off my boots and rested with my back against the wall. It was an effort to move as LP cooked and prepared for us. Kaman, our faithful porter, would get up and pick up the house water barrel and go off to some distant water supply and return with ten gallons on his back to tip into the family water bowl. I have often thought of that when I have been too tired to do something, yet had to fill the coal bucket, empty the bin, return to school for some meeting. Kaman would be my inspiration.

Thirst at altitude is all-consuming. With every step, I gasped and out came warm moist air, leaving me dehydrated to the point that it was the focus of all thoughts. At Lobuche we drank cup after cup of tea. In the tent I remember ensuring John had plenty to drink, mainly because that was all I could think about for myself. I certainly did not realise how vital it had been for John to rehydrate, and I often say a prayer of thanks that he suffered no greater problem than he did then, compared to events later in his life when he suffered two brain haemorrhages.

Back at Lobuche we found the Swiss couple had arrived. The tumbledown hut was full so we put up the tent for two to sleep in. I slept fitfully because of the altitude. Any movement woke me, gasping for breath and with a terrible headache. Even more difficult to contend with were the squeals and frantic scratching of the Swiss girl. She was covered in bed bug bites that were driving her demented. She scratched until she bled and squealed out in pain when the irritation became unbearable. Dawn, cold freezing dawn, was a blessed relief.

ഗ

John … It was strange how the altitude seemed to affect Johnny and me, since we considered ourselves to be the fittest. We had previously been to 15,000ft in the Alps and functioned quite well. We were 3,000ft higher than that here. We had been told by the New Zealand doctor at Khumjung to take much longer to ascend the 7,000ft from Namche, but we had neither the resources nor time to do that.

The last part of the walk on the 5th March, as we struggled to the top of Kala Pattar, had a dream-like quality for me. Not only was I fulfilling a dream, I was in one! It was like one of those dreams where you are trying to get somewhere but you never do. As a cross-country runner I had often pushed myself and felt exhausted, but never like this. I would take ten steps and then flop, totally 'done in'. Pam found it hard too, but not like me; in fact she had to wait for me.

As we approached the top I could see Dave and Johnny taking photos. Pam's camera was in Dave's rucksack and so I shouted to them to make sure she got it. There was no reply; they didn't even look in our direction. It wasn't windy and they were less than 30 yards away. It all added to the dream-like nature of the experience. When we reached the top they had gone. There was no sign of them, although we could see a long way and there was no place they could have been hidden from view. It was most strange.

When I think back and consider that unknown to me, there was an aneurysm in my brain I shudder to think what the outcome could have been. It burst for the first time four years later in 1972.

Wednesday 6ᵗʰ March, Day 17

A long, cold, sleepless night. I felt utterly tired, yet sleep did not come until I snatched two hours between 7.00pm and 9.00pm, then tossed and turned with a bad head until dawn at 5.30am. The Swiss girl had frenzies of scratching at the bed bugs' bites. Our superior friend, the Major, also had a bad head, which he could not understand. After all, he was no stranger to altitude, having been on Kilimanjaro in Africa some years ago.

The dawn was beautiful, heralding a similar day to yesterday. Both the other parties were heading for Kala Pattar as we began to descend. It took quite a time to pack, as our boots were frozen solid and the tent pegs were frozen into the ground. Pam's face and mine were sore from yesterday's sun. Bridal veils of snow were streaming from the peaks; there must be far more wind than yesterday. On the descent to Dingboche, another summer village, our heads kept turning to cast long glances back up the valley. A cold wind blew up, bringing much cloud with it.

The view down the valley from Lobuche. … '
The dawn was beautiful, heralding a day similar to yesterday'.

David …

Above Left: The hut at Lobuche 'was reminiscent of the Etchechan Bothy' in the Cairngorms, but with a hole in the roof'.

Above Right: Yak grazing in a frost glazed meadow at Pheriche under the towering presence of Kangtega and Tramserku.

Right: Cholatse (also known as Jobo Lhaptshan) towers above Pheriche – ' two or three stone huts'.

Right: David in Dingboche with Lhotse as a backdrop.

Far Right: Pam on the trail near Pheriche.

At Dingboche, a stark collection of dwellings like Pheriche, we had lunch of Sherpa potatoes. The lady of the house was busy with her chores, lugging wood and water about. There was a small child, only four days old, wrapped in skin at the fireside. Father sat outside, sewing in the sun. We were directly beneath Ama Dablam; up the valley we could see Lhotse and way above it the snow plume of Everest, drifting high on the gale-force winds that must have been blasting about the summit.

Down to Pangboche, then up the side of the valley to Tengboche. I was almost too tired to walk after three sleepless nights. Tengboche is a life-saver for it is so much lower in altitude at 12,715ft. We settled for the night in a house next to the monastery, although Pam and the old woman had to sleep in a house over the other side of the village – monastery rules. Only in special seasons can women sleep on the same side of the village as the monastery. John was a little better by evening. Johnny's feet are a real mess and he just cannot bear to have his boots on.

Since early afternoon, low cloud has blotted out everything. Yesterday was a blessing; now we can burst back to Kathmandu.

ও

Got up still feeling grotty. It was important that I got to a lower altitude as I was clearly suffering from mountain sickness. Followed the moraines, without my rucksack and wearing goggles as the sun was bright on the snow. Easy contouring path across sunlit meadows and then steeply down to Dingboche for dinner; fabulous potato stew. Still felt ill and weak, but a little better. Fine views of Lhotse. It was an easy afternoon walk to Pangboche and then up through a snow-filled forest to Tengboche. I was pleasantly surprised by my uphill performance. Slept in another good house in their 'prayer alcove' in a comfortable room. Pam had to sleep in another place as the house was in the monastery area.

John …

Spent the night in Tengboche Monastery, altitude 12,687ft.

11.5 miles; 262ft ascent; 3,750ft descent.

Memories 2010

We sat in the monastery completely exhausted, the four of us, our Sherpa and porter, and we were attended to by a group including an old woman, probably a nun. She seemed very old in her traditional costume and heavy shawl.

'In a house next to the monastery we settled for the night'.
Na Temba, with Johnny and John relaxing with some tea.

When LP told us that Pam could not sleep in the monastery we were a little apprehensive about letting her go off on her own. Women are not allowed to sleep on the same side of the plateau as the monastery building. In truth we had always felt safe on our journey and Pam herself certainly made no fuss. She went off into the darkness, armed with our only light, a bicycle lamp, following the old lady who was huddled in her shawl. They went to a typical Sherpa house, save this one had no animals downstairs and was completely empty upstairs except for two benches used as beds. She told me later how the old woman placed a yak skin over her sleeping bag and tucked her in as though she were a small child.

John …

Before going to sleep the eeriness of the situation increased as the woman chanted her prayers. She moved towards the open window and was silhouetted against the bright moonlit sky as she stood and prayed in a rhythmical chant. After kneeling and repeating her prayers she moved towards her bed. Pam, trying to be helpful, lit her way with the bike lamp. The woman gestured her disapproval and Pam realised that for centuries these people had moved around without the aid of artificial light and this strange intervention had disorientated her.

Later that night Pam awoke and realised she would have to get up to answer the call of nature. She made her way carefully to the door, down the ladder and through the outer doorway and described how the huge ghostly white shapes of the mountains actually startled her. They made her gasp audibly as she stepped out into the night, causing her to stumble backwards into the wall. The sky was filled with an inconceivably large array of stars and it was not hard to understand how this place was dedicated to the worship of a deity

I realise now that this was probably not the only situation where Pam, as the lone female on our trek, had to face problems that the rest of us didn't. She took it easily in her stride, never complained and showed great physical and mental courage.

The next night, in Namche Bazaar, with the call of nature equally pressing, Pam had to go outside again. She described moving cautiously to the ladder and down to the ground floor where about twenty yaks were housed. They shuffled, snuffled and lay in the darkness. Her eyes picked up the light of the moon coming through the open doorway. The warm breath of the yaks spiralled into the moonbeams as she picked her way through the animals. Once outside, the night was breathtaking in its brightness and beauty. The hanging glacier and snowfields shone with polished brilliance. The stars seemed close enough to touch and Pam's mind was overcome by the scale, the light and the mountains. There she was, a small person standing alone to witness that ethereal magnificence. Memories like this never fade.

Thursday 7ᵗʰ March, Day 18

A wonderful night's sleep in the small room that serves as a personal shrine to Buddha; the three of us slept soundly beneath his benign smile and the lights burning in his worship. Much refreshed we posed for last photographs before Everest. Then we turned our backs and headed back, away from the highest mountain in the world. We came back through Khumjung and its wonderful pattern of dry-stone walls.

David …

We visited the hospital financed by the New Zealand Sherpa Trust Fund. Dr John McKinnon was an excellent man, tremendously enthusiastic about his 3,000 patients. He has devised many schemes and conducted a few research schemes to aid the Sherpas. Smallpox, TB and goitre are the worst illnesses, plus others – burned children mainly. Also visiting him was an American doctor doing Peace Corps work in Central India. McKinnon's job seemed easy compared with the American's tales! Men like these give up prosperous jobs to help less fortunate nations, and Europeans should make more political capital out of this sort of behaviour instead of apologising for being successfully developed nations.

Very cold low cloud accompanied our return to Namche. Snow was just beginning to fall as we followed the steep path down through a maze of boulders.

Les has had a fine time in Namche. Kaman beamed to see us back. As we went to bed snow was falling heavily. The Sherpas told us that anything up to four feet may fall overnight!

❧

John ...

A lovely morning. Took group photographs with Everest in the background, before descending the steep slope to the river bed. Feeling much better at this lower altitude. Climbed better than expected up the other side of the valley to Khumjung. We walked through mist which had come down on the hanging valley of Khumjung, not sure whether or not the others had gone on to Khunde. We eventually heard their voices out of the mist and made our way to a house for dinner. Spent an hour or two with the New Zealand doctor. An American doctor arrived while we were there. Left for Namche in fog with a little drizzle, getting lost again in the boulders before wearily plodding to Namche. It snowed heavily in the night.

Spent the night in Namche Bazaar, altitude 11,289ft.

6 miles; 1,143ft ascent; 3,674ft descent.

Memories 2010

On my final day in Namche I walked up to Khunde to visit the New Zealand hospital and while I was there John and Dave arrived to return the maps they had borrowed from the doctor.

Les ...

The house I stayed in must have been one of the more prosperous ones in the village. It was stone-built with two storeys. The ground floor housed the animals – crossbreeds of half cow, half yak, called Dzos. The upper floor, which was reached by an internal staircase, housed the humans and was divided into two rooms. In one, the owner and his wife and small children lived and cooked over a smoky open fire. There were no toilet facilities and you made your own arrangements outside in the surrounding area or, in the case of the smallest child of the family, through the floorboards into the byre below.

When we returned to Nepal in 2010 the people explained to us that although attempts had been made to introduce chimneys they never caught on. The reasons they gave were that the smoke was useful for preserving food and it prevented insect attack on the timber of the building. The occupants were out working most of the day and when

Tengboche Monastery at dawn on 7th March.

they returned home they sat on the floor below the level of the smoke. Thus it was considered bearable, despite the obvious health risks.

The walls were lined with shelves holding brass and copper storage vessels and aluminium cooking pots. The only light during the day was from a tiny window and at night from small tapers made from split wood wedged between the stones of the wall. They burnt for a few seconds but long enough for the person to move from the fireside to the storage shelves. The other room held more storage containers and was also the sleeping quarters of the schoolteacher and any guests who might arrive.

While we were there a party of Canadians arrived, having flown in to Lukla. I felt very superior, having walked from Dolalghat. I spent some time drawing the interior and when we came home I used the drawings to make the painting reproduced in this book.

Slow 35mm colour film meant that our hand held shots lack definition but they show great detail of life in a Sherpa house.

A woman with a 'back warmer' attends to household chores. The 'water rucksack' can be seen on the floor and a leg of meat hangs from the ceiling. Large pots for storing water sit on shelves marked with dabs of paint.

Children having a warm drink sitting on one of the few beds we saw. There was actually glass in the window in this house! A fire burned brightly as breakfast was cooking.

Les's painting
made from a sketch
done in 'situ'.
It shows the
interior of the
house where we
stayed in Namche
Bazaar.

Chapter 8

Home Kaman and
Don't Spare the Sherpa

Friday 8th March, Day 19

There were about four inches of snow outside as we prepared to leave Namche. We all seemed relieved at the prospect of returning, which will take about ten more days. In the soft, wet snow we set out. Kaman was barefoot again. He probably sold his outsize plimsolls in Namche.

All the way down 'Namche Hill', a steep drop of about 500ft, the path was slippery with melting snow. As we left the big mountains behind, pine trees shuddered off their overnight covering and drips pattered in the forests. I halted for a short while at the last place from which I could see Everest. Over the Nuptse Ridge the hog's back of the 29,000ft mountain was just visible as cloud scuttled in to hide it.

We wanted to reach LP's father's village for evening. This meant a long day and we were continually changing our dress as the hot sun alternated with cold cloud.

We are running short of Nepalese rupees, but LP intends to borrow some or to change some of our Indian rupees in his home village. On arriving at his grandfather's house – half an hour in front of LP who was hoping to slow-time us for a stay at Ang Temba's – we found his grandmother seriously ill. So we had to stay with LP's aunt; it seems the whole village is related. A brisk shower of rain freshened up the atmosphere; I could smell the freshly-ploughed fields.

David ...

Namche nestled into the hillside, viewed from the path down the valley.

Down in the valleys we are back among bird life and flowers. Appetites are enormous and we cannot be filled. I suspect we have all lost weight on the trek. We talked of fantastic menus for an eating orgy we planned for our return to Kathmandu.

John ... We awoke to find four inches of snow outside, and fantastic views and atmosphere. We got on the road, eager to make early progress on our way back to Kathmandu. We now just wanted to get back to rest and good food. The path was snow-covered and yet Kaman wore no shoes. Descended slowly with Pam. As snow dripped from the glistening trees around us, I returned several times to the viewpoint for one last look at Everest. I could hardly pull myself away.

When we reached the valley bottom, the snow thinned out and walking became easier. Kept going fairly well all day, with rain in the late afternoon. We arrived at LP's father's place which had been the one and a half day point on the outward journey. We were running short of money, but LP said he could get some here. I hoped he could, otherwise we would be going hungry.

March 8th, leaving Namche Bazar in four inches of snow.

Spent the night at LP's grandfather's in Nangbug (near Lukla), at altitude 8,530ft.

11 miles; 1,312ft ascent; 3,806ft descent.

Saturday 9th March, Day 20

David ...

Great fun all day. LP was missing at breakfast, which was ominous after our last stay at Nangbug. Kaman prepared breakfast. LP was collecting rupees that some part of the family owed him. As the women paid him, a family row blew up, and that involved a man threatening a woman with a large block of wood.

We left LP trying to settle the row and for four hours we punished ourselves up a very steep hill and down the other side, then up the next hill, laboriously trying to reach a spot we had chosen for lunch. Then we had to wait for three hours for LP to catch up. We ate a scratch meal without utensils, which he was carrying. When he did arrive, it was as we feared: he was drunk again. Not able to make any sense of him, especially as he refused to come on, we dismissed him.

As Johnny shared out LP's load we realised he was not carrying anything like the amount he should have been. Without him, we sped on to Rai Sherpa's village. Kaman asked for a 20 rupee bonus, which

121

Above Left: David and Pam on the path down from Namche, 'snow covered and yet Kaman wore no shoes'.

Above Right: 'I took a last look at Everest, but returned to the viewpoint several times for one last look as snow dripped from the glistening trees'.

John ...

we readily agreed to. Kaman chose a thatched shelter for our night's lodging – merely a thatched roof on six supports.

Kaman took charge of fire arrangements and we took charge of the food and supplies. Strange how we all feel better now that we are in command of the situation. Following LP was not always easy. Now we dictate meals, distance and so on, whereas if we tried to do so before, LP hid behind a "not understand" wall.

୬

It was late in the morning when LP arrived, having slept elsewhere, but he had 180 rupees. So we should be OK. I stuck my head out of the house window this morning and heard a bird singing. It brought back vivid pictures of an English pastoral scene and for a moment I felt quite homesick. Set off up the steep climb with Pam, and going quite well until we reached a col.

We went down from there and up the other side to another col where we found the others waiting for dinner. We did the cooking ourselves as LP hadn't arrived. When he finally caught us up, two and a half hours later and obviously drunk, I had words with him and he refused to go on. We sacked him and gave Kaman a one-rupee rise. LP's rucksack contained very little and we shared that out between us.

As we plodded down from that col I had a feeling of insecurity: we were still eight to ten days from Kathmandu without a guide, but it gave the venture a new and exciting air. Down, down and down past Khari Khola and, with Kaman agreeable, on again to Rai Sherpa's. Pam and I arrived almost at dusk. I had a much-needed wash and sat down to a blow-out prepared by Johnny and Kaman. This was not really a Sherpa village, but a Nepalese one. There was a fabulous atmosphere with the open fire making silhouettes of bamboos and banana trees. The moon above, the mountains steep and high, and us sleeping in an open-sided barn. Although we had learned valuable things from LP, it felt much more adventurous without him. A strange feeling of being free to do as we wished.

Spent the night at Rai Sherpa's near Jubing, altitude 5,128ft.

13 miles; 3,543ft ascent; 5,643ft descent.

Memories 2010

When LP got drunk yet again, we bubbled and burned until we burst out in anger. We talked about it for several hours before agreeing to leave him behind. Kaman was a kind gentleman, who not only saw more money for himself but who also wanted to care for us. He knew the problem and never joined LP in any of the drinking or slow-timing.

David ...

We were ravenously hungry as we surged on towards Kathmandu. We were consuming vast quantities of rice but our bodies used up the calories very quickly, and craved salt and flavour. Each night we rubbed some gritty rock salt on a serrated stone, scattering the granules over the rice. For more flavour, we added raw red chilli pepper to the mounds of rice. When we had curry or meat there was only a very small amount compared to the rice.

But although I dreamt about food I never allowed myself to join in the more public debates about what we would eat when we could – chocolate digestive biscuits, chips and egg and other favourite dishes. I felt it would lower, rather than raise my morale. Johnny could talk at length of what he was missing, what he wished he had, what he would like, how he hated the monotonous diet. But for me all that did was take away the resolve to succeed. I did not join in and probably seemed detached, but it was to protect myself from the weaknesses of the flesh.

∽

John ... It was only after we had finally had our fill of LP's drunkenness and sacked him that we realised he had just lent us all the rupees we possessed. I still marvel at our audacity. It was really our only complaint with his service and he made no effort to be awkward with us or to demand his money back. We had dollars with us but we had underestimated how many rupees we would need to take with us on the trek. We repaid him in Kathmandu.

Sunday 10th March, Day 21

David ... After a good night under our shelter we continued down through the rhododendron woods to the bottom of the Dudh Kosi. Many trees are a blaze of scarlet flowers. Going up the other side was hard work in the tropical atmosphere. This was the first side of the three big ridges we must cross.

Our first lunch without a Sherpa was great. We stopped in a clearing near a cowherd's summer quarters, looking back over the great white range. Johnny took charge of cooking as we dried out in the sun.

Describing the afternoon session as 'a long uphill' is not sufficient. It went up and up through damp forests until at last we emerged on the col. After a rum fudge treat it was a quick descent through primula-covered alps to reach our stop for the night. A luxury of a banana each to eat for pudding.

∽

John ... Got up at the crack of dawn, with Kaman already tending the fire and putting the kettle on. I helped him make the porridge and we were away much earlier than usual. Down to cross the Namche

River for the last time. Up steeply on the other side, our biggest 'graunch' on the way home. Passed where we spent a night on the outward journey and on to a grassy alp for dinner. It was great cooking in the open – no payments for firewood and much pleasanter. We had a big meal, as much as we wanted. I think that after a whole day we are better off without LP. After dinner we made good progress to the first ridge where we had rum fudge. From here we could see the Sherpa house where we were to sleep.

Pam set off down quickly and I followed. She went well, again without a stop, up the other side to the house. Johnny had organised the stop before Kaman arrived. I was now convinced we could manage better without LP. We indulged in another ace meal, with bananas for pudding. It was good to get away from the usual LP recipes.

'Our first lunch without a Sherpa was great. We stopped in a clearing, looking back over the great white range'.

Spent the night at Salung, altitude 9,790ft.
10 miles; 6,168ft ascent; 1,939ft descent.

Memories 2010

David ...

We bought a large aluminium kettle in Kathmandu to use on the trek and it was invaluable for boiling the large quantities of water we needed for tea at every stop. After every meal it was black from sitting in the fire, but Kaman never failed to restore its shine. In the house he wet his hands and used wood ash from the fireplace as an abrasive powder. With practised ease he scoured the surface with his hand and this home-made 'Vim'. He rinsed off the paste and put the kettle on top of his basket. When we cooked out in the hills and woods, Kaman then took the blackened kettle to the nearby stream and cupped a handful of sand and gravel to give the surface a real polish. It had been done that way for hundreds of years.

Monday 11th March, Day 22

David ... Long traverse and descent to the village of Junbesi, through fields full of primula, their purple haze so refreshing. We bought rice and sugar at a very clean house with a proper bed and mattress, even sleeping clothes and good equipment. One of the children was scolded for having dirty hands.

Our route then took us up and up then for about one and half hours. To break the long ascent we stopped in the woods for a lunch of boiled eggs and chapatti. It was then an awful slog uphill for almost two hours before reaching the cold col that led to the snow traverse, which I really hated as it prevented rapid movement. It took four hours going down through occasional rain to Kenja.

❧

John ... We set off along the beautiful and easy path to Junbesi. I got a last view of Everest. This surprised me because LP had said it couldn't be seen from here. It took an hour to reach Junbesi (I lost my Outward Bound Trust badge there on the way out), where Dave, Johnny and Kaman bought rice and sugar. We stopped for lunch half an hour later in another smashing spot. Dave cooked chapattis and I boiled eggs. We made it easily up to the second ridge top in an hour, with Pam going very well. As we crossed a stretch of snow her ankle began to hurt – the going was very slow now. The ridge down which we were going had been the highest on the way out and Pam found it difficult to manage the descent; it took nearly four hours to reach the bottom.

Meanwhile we experienced occasional thundery showers accompanied by sharp flashes of lightning. We were very thankful to get to the bottom as darkness fell and a vicious storm broke; it was certainly a good job we were off the hill. We slept in a newly built house with four Sherpanis – apparently someone had tried to kick us out but had been told what to do. There was another good big meal and we got to sleep as the storm abated.

Spent the night at Kenja, altitude 5,249ft.

13 miles; 3,412ft ascent; 6,233ft descent.

Tuesday 12th March, Day 23

David …

When we came to leave there was trouble over money. The man refused our notes. He even charged for the loan of a bowl, but did not think that half the firewood we had paid for being returned meant a discount.

It was steeply downhill as we made a big push for Barikharga (Bhandar). We tried every house that we passed for eggs. The sun was very hot. Steady uphill for one hour to the third big col before charging down the valley to Those. We slept in the roughest house in this quaint village.

❧

John …

It was a beautiful morning. I cooked breakfast and then we were off down the valley. An hour and a half later we started up the steep hill to Barikharga. It was very hot and Pam was not going so well. I was surprised by the shortness of the hill and then we went over flatter land to the village for dinner. Another great dinner and then I sent Pam on ahead; I caught her up half-way to the top. Barikharga was on a beautiful Alpine-like meadow and I shall always retain fond memories of good food there. We made the top quite easily and this was the last of the three big ridges.

'We had lunch of boiled eggs and Chapatti, in the woods'.

Going down the other side, I stayed behind with Pam and I gloated over the fact that we were going down over the ground that we had previously climbed in a great 'thrutch'. At the bottom we followed the beautiful river valley down to Those. On the way we stopped to watch a wedding celebration. Darkness was falling as we slowly approached the village. We found the others upstairs in the residence of the 'Cougher Royal', where we had lunch on the way out. Had a chat with a Sherpa downstairs who gave us a water purifier which had been given to him by a German. He said the route via Barahbesi was one day shorter, but Kaman was not really in favour and I preferred to stick to the track I know.

Spent the night in Those, altitude 5,709ft.

12 miles; 3,625ft ascent; 3,232ft descent.

Memories 2010

David ...   One very hot day I was consumed by thirst. I was walking with John along a terrace quite near a village. A spring ran out of the bank at the side of the path. It was channelled into a split bamboo spout and the bright clear water cascaded over the end to form a running waterfall. I stopped and wiped my brow. I cupped my hands and washed my face. John did the same. At that point I had not drunk any unboiled water throughout the trek. We debated whether there was any truth in the fact that fast flowing spring water could not be contaminated. I wet my lips. I then drank a deliciously cool mouthful to slake my thirst. I felt better but I worried for hours that some deadly waterborne disease would liquefy my insides. Eventually, when nothing happened, I forgave myself for my indulgence but I did not try it again.

Somewhere along the trek we went down to the river to wash. We didn't wash very frequently and we were dirty and sweaty. I like to be organised so I had my toilet bag with the soapbox and toothpaste. I had a really good strip wash and felt all the better for it. Johnny came later and asked to borrow my soap. It was balanced on a rock and I left him to it. He needed a good wash because he neither changed nor washed any garment during the month. He returned without the soap or the box. I made a quick walk to the river but someone had beaten me to it.

Wednesday 13ᵗʰ March, Day 24

David ...   We walked along the valley over the spur, then upstream to the bridge, where we had lunch at the bottom of the steep hill. Last lunch of egg and chapatti because there is no flour left. Uphill was hard work in the hot sun; many rhododendrons in flower. On the top we could see over to Namdu and Katakuti. Then it was down a long

'It was good to be back in Namdu, a very pleasant village'. We slept in the shelter next to the house on the way out and in the shelter in the fore-ground (next to the pig-sty) on our return.

contour across the hill to Namdu. LP appeared and we were rather worried, but he slept elsewhere and we learned that he was returning quickly to Kathmandu. We were relieved at this for we are happier without him. We are rather filthy and welcomed having a big wash at the river. It was good beneath a full moon.

Another nice morning with a beautiful walk down a valley and then over a spur. Up the next valley, passing the village where we had spent the night on the way out, and then it was on to the foot of the steep climb over to Namdu.

John ...

A good dinner, but the weather was very hot and we dreaded the climb. At midday, after Pam had stalled a little, we set off half an hour after the others. I persuaded Pam to let me carry her rucksack and we left at a good pace. There was no stopping us and we passed Kaman, Dave, Les and, surprising, Johnny, when we reached the top. It was a great relief to think that the last of the really big hills was behind us.

Down pleasantly to a resting spot near an outward dinner stop. Here we looked up and saw LP coming down with a sheepish grin on his face. He gave us some excuse about the earlier incident and then followed us on the easy ground to Namdu. We wondered on the way down whether he expected to be taken on again. I rushed on with the others, leaving Pam, in order to 'sort out' LP. When he arrived at Namdu he simply went to another house. He had made us feel uneasy during the last hour or so, thinking that he might influence Kaman, but fortunately had not. It was good to be back in Namdu, a very pleasant village, feeling almost home now. Great sense of relief and wellbeing. Almost too hot at night.

Spent the night in Namdu, altitude 4,724 ft.

12 miles; 3,412ft ascent; 3,018ft descent.

Thursday 14ᵗʰ March, Day 25

David ...   From Namdu the path went down steeply to the river valley. Near the river there was a cremation ceremony taking place, with horns being blown and singing. Uphill to take an early lunch at 'Two Trees Col'. Here we asked Kaman to find out the route to Barahbesi, which was one day away. Dolalghat is two and a half days away and it would be wonderful to save a day on the route. Johnny is having a down-in-the-mouth phase, depressing everybody; Les same as ever, hating every step. John and I accept the trudge and enjoy the 'exercise'. So we decided to try the Barahbesi route to get back quicker. Kaman claimed not to know the way. Johnny chased around the two shops asking for information.

A long drag in the afternoon with far too many rests. Pam is going very slowly. I'm tired, but happy. Contoured round from the two trees until we reached the river and followed it to where the valleys meet. There in a small village was a very strange building that looked just like a Methodist chapel. Women sat around smoking, taking a bit of tobacco, then looking around for a suitable dry leaf with which to roll the a cigarette. A small girl sat among them, maybe seven or eight years old, smoking too.

One hour up the valley there were ominous rumblings of thunder. The first house could not accommodate us. The second house agreed to have lodgers at a reasonable price. We moved in just as the storm broke. Wonderful skies full of greys and blacks that were shattered occasionally by lightning. There is talk of Les and Johnny going on ahead tomorrow to get the Land Rover. Not much point really if the rest of us don't get there until following day, but it will please them, so we are happier all round tonight.

৯

A hot night but I didn't sleep too badly. We set off down a gentle slope, which then steepened down to the river, where Pam and I had a wash stop. Earlier in the morning a funeral procession had passed us and they were cremating the body about 100 yards upstream. The atmosphere was really tropical, with chattering birds and gaudy flowers. Going up the other side of the valley seemed easier than we had expected, except towards the top. The weather was very hazy and Gauri Sankar was barely visible.

At the top, by the two trees, we found the others having the dinner stop. There was talk again of the quicker route via Barahbesi; apparently they had met LP who had said he would be in Kathmandu by three the following day. Johnny and Les were very keen to take the shorter route (Johnny declared that he had hated every minute of the trip and seemed depressed about it). I preferred to go the way I knew and it would only make one day's difference. Johnny established which way to go, got Kaman to agree, and so we set off on the different route.

There was an initial upward traverse to the corner and then a downward one to the river valley. It was very hot and Pam's feet were troubling her again. I hated being in a position of not knowing where I was going. It was slow going up the valley – I took Pam's rucksack again – then it was over a rickety bridge to a village where the others were waiting.

We had one more hour of steep going, up a valley to Surki, where we were refused at one house but accepted at the next, just as a storm broke over us. It soon abated and we were able to cook outside. That night there was talk of two of us pushing on ahead to Kathmandu to

John ...

'The atmosphere was really tropical'. John pauses on the path having just crossed the Likhu Kohla.

131

"After 27 days we caught our first glimpse of a road with a jeep travelling along it; what a moment, this spurred us on".

David …

organise the Land Rover, etc, but I was against the idea as I would have preferred us to arrive back together, as a team. But team spirit now seemed to be non-existent and there was an atmosphere of 'let's get the hell out of here'. Morale was flagging at a time when we should have been elated. It was like being with a bad patrol at Ullswater, when those around me are contemptuous of what I hold dear. Only Dave and I were quietly contented with our achievements so far and were enjoying its final moments with satisfaction.

Spent the night in Surki.

Friday 15th March, Day 26

Les and Johnny left early for the dash to Kathmandu. A cloudy, yellow and beautiful dawn before the plod uphill; Pam moving very slowly. At 9.30am we sat on the top. We thought the time given to us to be an over-estimate; after all, we had only downhill to go. Finding water is a problem, with no streams on the high ridge. We had lunch at 11.30am near a house where there was a badly burned child. We presume he must have fallen into the open fire. We offered a tube of antiseptic cream and he was soon smothered in that. We are not sure what good it will do, with flies crawling all over his flesh. Down, down the ridge to Balebi.

After a good lunch we headed along the ridge and descended as quickly as possible, keeping our heads down in a storm. Fortunately the worst of the storm followed the ridge opposite. Far below us we saw the road and that gave us new energy. We had to cross the last swaying suspension bridge at about 4.30pm to find there was no bus until 6.00am next day. Completely deflated we crawled on to yet another veranda beneath a very bright full moon.

ॐ

Les and Johnny left early as planned; the rest of us followed on half an hour later. The track rose gently up the valley and finally more steeply to the col. From here I could see the lie of the land and understood our position in relation to Risingo and Dolalghat. The track continued along the level through villages and maize fields, then over forested ground and steeply down a ridge to where we had dinner.

The track continued to contour the hills and was remarkably well-engineered. As we slowly descended, the sky clouded over and it began to rain. We caught our first glimpse of the road with a jeep travelling along it – what a moment! It spurred us on.

Kaman stopped and told us that there was a bus at 5.00pm. His English was certainly getting better. It was great to think that we would be in Kathmandu that night. Just before reaching the road we had to cross the most rickety and dangerous bridge of the whole journey. As I staggered on to the road I was greeted with the news that there was, in fact, no bus. We walked a mile or so further to Balebi where we hung around a teashop in the hope that there might be some passing vehicle which would take us to Kathmandu.

As dusk fell we resigned ourselves to a night out at Balebi and

'Just before reaching the road we had to cross the most rickety and dangerous bridge of the whole journey'.

John ...

we followed Kaman to a house. It had a bit of a grotty veranda but they put down a very nice mat for us. Kaman, Pam and I helped with the cooking, while Dave entertained a whole crowd of villagers by writing his log.

What a let-down, having the 'carrot' of comfort and good food in Kathmandu whipped away at the last moment. Where were the other two? Perhaps in Kathmandu enjoying a fine nosh while we ate a meat bar? Or, alternatively, sitting starving somewhere up the road? The moon shone faintly through a layer of clouds, the crickets chirped and the night air was warm and very damp.

Spent the night in Balebi.

Memories 2010

Pam half way across, where the bridge swings most and David waiting to cross this last hurdle before 'civilisation'.

David ...

The bus was long gone and we were on a veranda above the road looking out over the valley. I lay on a mat facing the clear sky and the brightest moon I have ever experienced. I was quite overcome with the bright white light and the face of the moon. I was transfixed by the immensity of it all and the clarity of space, but it could not diminish what I felt I had achieved. I remember vividly the black sky and the intensely bright moon, as I lay awake enjoying the pleasure of my achievement. Not much was said because the sense of pride was masked by tiredness, an aching leg and some sense of apprehension about Les and Johnny and their dash for Kathmandu.

ക

Les ...

We set off back to Dolalghat. I enjoyed the return trip far more than the trek out. Possibly, it was the tantalising prospect of the Everest Restaurant or even the cold shower in the Camp Hotel. Mainly though it was because I was now fit and rested and could romp across the hills like a mountain goat. So much so that, rather selfishly in retrospect, Johnny and I split the party on the penultimate day, and made a dash for the road, thus arriving in Kathmandu a day earlier than the others. Our excuse was that we could collect the Land Rover, re-establish ourselves in the Camp Hotel and have everything ready for the return of the others. In truth, I was a bit frustrated at the slow progress we were making, not realising how exhausted Pam was after 27 days of continuous trekking.

Saturday 16th March, Day 27

David ...

Kaman, prompt as ever, woke me excitedly, saying "Sahib, Sahib, bus come." Below us at the barrier, brightly lit in the still dark morning, was a bus. Even Pam needed no second call to rise. We packed and dashed down to have tea before boarding our chariot. I did not have insufficient rupees for the fare but the neat little conductor said I could pay on arrival in Kathmandu – so accommodating to Sahibs. Later he offered to change a dollar for ten rupees, before finally agreeing to give me 12 rupees.

As 6.00am we roared off amid great horn blaring. Our trek was over. A polo-neck-jerseyed driver flung the bus along, scaring us at every hairpin. Time couldn't be that valuable? Thirty-five minutes later we skidded on to the bridge at Dolalghat. Thankful for the pause, we got out for another glass of tea. Both drivers began their second business, buying firewood, chickens and fish. We sat staring through the steady rain at the steep path where we had begun one month earlier. Thank goodness we were not trekking in this steady downpour. Our minds ran back over the 27 days of our trek, the experiences, the joys, the hard work, sweat and dirt. All was behind us: we were nearly home.

Two and a half hours later we lurched to a halt. Johnny greeted us and led the way to the 'New Tibetan' for our first reward of tea and toast. Four rounds of that, while we got the details of Johnny and Les's push yesterday. They reached Kathmandu too late to do anything except book in at The Camp. Les arrived after getting the Land Rover. Pity it was Saturday, because the post office was closed.

Back at The Camp we bedded down after ordering hot water. Johnny prepared our second reward: chips, fried eggs, tomatoes and bread, so delicious. After a bath and a good meal we had a walk, savouring the city atmosphere, so quaint and far removed from home, yet feeling like a city after our 28 days in the hills. Here were fresh vegetables, sugar, eggs, masses of shops and people, newspapers, cars, temples, other Europeans, and our dear Land Rover. My leg was painful and swollen; thank goodness it went on the last day.

At 6.30pm, starving, we entered the 'Everest' and ordered three Chinese dinners and five plates. Their reputation was justified. First a large bowl of meat and noodle soup, second a bowl of fried rice and bits, plus a meat and a savoury pancake. We waded slowly through the pile. Johnny was defeated and left us to enjoy another tiny pancake and coffee. Not quite satiated, we retired to The Camp restaurant for tea and another pancake and jam. Thoroughly bunged at the beginning of our resting orgy we went to bed.

৯

John ... "**S**ahib, bus." I looked up and there at the corner was an illuminated bus. We packed quickly and made our way down for a quick cup of tea before boarding the bus. The fare was 6.50 rupees, almost double that from Dolalghat. Fortunately the fare collector was prepared to accept one US dollar as 12 rupees. The weather was still cloudy as the bus drove off. Half-way to Dolalghat the drivers changed and a maniac took over, who absolutely terrified me on the final hill, skidding as he turned to take the bridge at the bottom. More tea here and it began to rain heavily.

The roads were wet and I was beginning to wish I had walked to Kathmandu. On a rough patch that the driver took at a ridiculous speed, the bus took quite a battering. I think it shocked him, as from then on he drove more steadily. We had more frustrating stops, notably at Banepa, before reaching a rain-soaked Kathmandu, to find Johnny waiting for us.

Johnny and Les had arrived the night before. We went straight to the New Tibetan for the tea and toast we had promised ourselves. We later met Les who had been to retrieve the Land Rover and had lost my visiting card at the same time. Then back to The Camp where

Wash day in Patan.

rooms had been booked. We paid off Kaman and LP. I had a good wash in hot water and then Johnny cooked a welcome meal of fried eggs and tomatoes. We spent the afternoon lying about and getting hungry.

At 6.30pm we went to the Everest Restaurant. There we ordered three Chinese meals between us and it was soon apparent that there would be ample - dish after dish of exotic mixtures appeared until we were completely bunged. I had to take a walk and Johnny, who left to go home, was sick. We followed this up by two-thirds of a pancake and then went to the Camp restaurant to finally seal our fate with another pancake. I suffered all night with indigestion.

The trek was an experience I would not have missed for the world but I doubt if I would again attempt such a journey. It took more out of us than we realised. In the 27 days I have lost over a stone in weight, but I am fitter than I have been since my school days. I can appreciate the comforts of civilisation with far more feeling. The overall, over-riding sensation is that I have seen the greatest peak on earth, Mount Everest, 29,002ft.

Johnny ...

137

John ... We had achieved our ambition and returned without mishap, to enjoy the comforts that Kathmandu offered. The whole 27-day trek had, somewhat incredibly, cost just over £33 for all of us (£7 each for 27 days trekking!), a sum which also included the pay for our Sherpa and porter. We needed to rest, write home and prepare for our return.

Chapter 9

Return to India and Home

Sunday 17th March

First the mail: what a delight it is to receive mail from home. After much shopping, we returned to have our breakfast of eggs, bread and tomatoes and cornflakes.

David ...

My leg seemed worse so I strapped it up, promising to rest it. For dinner I cooked chips, eggs and beans, tea, bread and real butter. The water was off, so we had to have it much later than planned. Bunged again, we lay around until John cooked pancakes, served with sugar and lemons

Rain fell heavily amid thunderstorms. What of those in hills?

Full stomachs bade us goodnight to sleep deeply until 6.00am. Habits take some breaking. Tried to write letters, but I am still too exhausted to think clearly, to be able to sort out sensibly from the mass of a month's experience.

❧

Up early after an uncomfortable night due to indigestion. Dave and I went on a shopping trip, which took an hour and a half, for enough materials for another day's eating orgy. We ended up at the Post Office and received piles of letters. We couldn't read them straight away as our hands were full. While Dave cooked the full works for breakfast we all sat around reading letters and soaking up news from home. A really great breakfast after which we sat around a little bloated again. We met LP and Kaman during the morning and LP bought us

John ...

A simple footbridge over the river just below the Camp Hotel.

an orange each – perhaps a bit of a peace offering?

Later in the afternoon Dave cooked the eggs, chips and beans we had promised ourselves. Another great success, but we realised there wasn't time for another big meal that day. Les and I played cards as the weather was still a bit damp; it reminded us of a wet Saturday afternoon at home. About 9.00pm I cooked pancakes for everyone and this finally 'bound our clacks', and gave me indigestion for yet another night. I went to pick up my 35mm films from the Foreign Post in the afternoon; got them with relatively little fuss. A great load off my mind. A great relaxing day and what a change after a month's solid trekking.

Memories 2010

David ... Life back in Kathmandu seemed very civilised compared to life in the hill villages. There was a shower room and a toilet, which was a bare concrete room with a hole in the floor. It was not a pleasant place to be. A rat appeared up the hole one day when I was in there. Cockroaches marched across in ranks. The rooms were entirely bare and primitive but the restaurant was heaven for pancakes and tea. It was small and warm and there was a buzz of conversation.

I was resting and unable to walk. Johnny went out shopping and came back with the essentials but he was eating a bar of chocolate! He gave each one of us a square. It was delicious but it was against the expedition's financial policy!

ॐ

John …

Les and I were walking to the British Embassy when we met Kaman in the street. This was some days after the end of the trek. We greeted each other with warmth and affection, but there the conversation pretty much ended, as understanding was limited to "Are you OK?" I don't think I have ever wanted to be able to speak another man's language more than at that moment. We knew him so well and were so fond of him, but in all probability we would never see him again. How inadequate it was simply to smile at him and give him the thumbs-up as we went our separate ways.

In fact, just a few years later three of us, quite independently, saw him on television working as a porter on a Bonington expedition.

Monday 18th March

David …

Definitely a rest day for my leg. I have not been on my feet since I cooked breakfast. Still very tired and content to laze around. The trip took far more out of us than we realised. My great problem, I think, was lack of sound sleep because my hips stick out too much to use the ground as a mattress. Our camp beds are idyllic; we have always thought so, but now we are convinced. Letter writing is an awful problem and I dashed off two that were most unsatisfactory – there's far too much to tell all at once.

Apart from resting and writing, I have eaten great quantities of food. The dinner menu was cheese, tomatoes, bread and butter, fruit salad and custard. For tea, fried goat meat and onions, mashed potato, cabbage, rice pudding. In between, coffee and biscuits kept hunger at bay.

Pam lost her engagement ring: a sad blow. She left it in the bathroom after washing her hair and we feared that someone had stolen it. No amount of asking and searching and bringing in the police has retrieved it.

ॐ

Woodcutters provide the fuel for the city.

John ... Another bad night. The morning was a bit rainy again. Les and I shopped for breakfast and then went to the British Embassy. There were no letters there for Les, who had had none from the post office, nor anyone else. We called in at the British Council Library and the post office on the way back. Missed a very heavy shower while reading newspapers in the library.

We returned to another fine meal of cheese (what a luxurious taste, the first decent cheese since Turkey), tomatoes, bread and butter, followed by fresh fruit salad and custard.

Pam then gave me the awful news that she had lost her engagement ring. I can write dispassionately about it now, as it has been found, but at the time I felt positively sick. She left it in the bathroom and returned ten minutes later to find it gone. The Camp management did all they could. A little kid even felt down the bogs! I felt sure it had been 'lifted' and lost for good. We went around asking everybody and then went to the police station to report the loss. A constable came back with us and he had a little poke about, but that was all: we could do no more than hope.

Les cooked goat meat for tea very successfully and we all ate rather less to avoid indigestion. I wrote letters and cards, but couldn't get the ring off my mind. Pam and I talked for some time about how we should replace it, if at all, but got so depressed that we decided to leave it for a few days, hoping that it might turn up. Just before going

142

Sherpanis bringing firewood wood supplies to the city, after several days walk from their village.

to bed the bearded chap in the office gave us new hope by saying that the drains would be searched next day. A better night's sleep but the ring rather dwelt on my mind.

Tuesday 19th March

David ...

Another very restful day eating and trying to fill in my expedition log. Breakfast over, I sat and wrote all morning as Johnny shopped. For lunch, delightful fresh bread and butter and banana fritters and custard, another successful addition to our menus.

Reading, writing and resting all afternoon. Evening meal a success save for John's rolled rice sauce, one of his less successful creations. Apart from that I never left the room. Pam got her ring back.

John ...

Got up and went to buy bread, milk, eggs etc. for breakfast. When I returned, Pam announced that her ring had been found. The boy who had found it had gone out for the day, but brought it back later. What a relief. I suddenly felt happy again.

After breakfast Pam and I went to the post office in hot sun. It seemed so bright after the last few days and we felt very lethargic.

Above Left: Basantapur Square, 'it must have been market day'.

Above Right: The barber's shop at the top of the road from the Camp Hotel.

Left: The Hanuman Dhoka Palace.

Below Left: Degutaleju Temple in the centre of Kathmandu.

Below Right: Hanuman Dhoka Road in Kathmandu, 'like the 'Shambles' in medieval York'.

Upon our return we were absolutely exhausted and I spent the rest of the morning catching up with this log. After dinner I wrote a number of postcards and then went shopping with Pam for the evening meal. We bought some rolled rice to make a pudding. I cooked and made successful savoury pancakes, but the 'coffee crisp' pudding was less so.

We had spent three days now doing very little, and although I thought that we deserved it, I knew that I should begin to feel guilty if we didn't do something within the next few days. I hoped to visit a school the next day and see some of the sights we had missed on our outward journey. There was a very relaxed atmosphere in Kathmandu and you could understand why some people seemed to stay so long.

We met the Liverpudlians that night; they were in the process of selling their van. (On the outward journey near Trabson in Turkey we met a young couple from Liverpool with a small child of about four years old. They were travelling in a Ford Thames Van and we met them again by chance in the streets of Kathmandu. They were selling their van so they could fly home.)

Wednesday 20ᵗʰ March

Feeling much better. After a leisurely morning I even had sufficient energy to go shopping and take some photographs of this remarkable city. I hadn't been out long when a thunderstorm broke. There seems to be one, late every afternoon at this time of year. I sat for shelter in a stationery shop after buying some airmail paper. Outside in the steady rain porters ran to and fro with sacks on their backs. Another group sat near a pile of corrugated metal sheeting waiting to move it.

David …

As the sun broke through, I wandered down the old back streets, catching some of the atmosphere on film. A large black bull nosed his way through the vegetable market, snaffling what he could. As I stood watching, each stall holder threw a handful of leaves to him. Such a venerated creature is certainly well fed. People pushed up to touch him, others bent their heads to touch him. Strange. Behind him limped a calf with a broken leg that had been bound with filthy sacks.

An evening meal of cheese salad was perfect. I spent the night writing to *The Barnsley Chronicle*.

John ...   Breakfast was a little late again. I didn't accomplish as much as I had expected, spending part of the morning finishing the 25 postcards I was going to send, then going to the American Library to read some books on Everest. I have been suffering very badly from indigestion lately: it makes meals an unpleasant time, though goodness knows I've been getting enough down me.

Spent most of the afternoon writing to Dave Harbour. He had been the sixth member of our party, saving and planning for two years with the rest of us. Unfortunately he broke his femur in a skiing accident and had to withdraw from the expedition at a late stage. We took it in turns to write to him and keep him informed of our progress.

As nobody else seemed to want to visit the school, I resolved that the next day I would go on my own if the others still showed the same reluctance. (As we were all teachers we obviously had an interest in schools and visited a number on our travels.)

Planned the next day a little more precisely: it was to be our last day so we just had to get things done. I was now getting rather bored and would be glad to be on the move again. We were all fully rested now.

❧

Johnny ...   A day similar to yesterday with nothing of importance to do except general activities. The day drifted by as most days in Kathmandu seem to do. The city has a strange sort of timelessness about it and I find it difficult even to walk quickly along the streets. Apart from that, I am beginning to feel extremely fit. The large quantities of food we are eating are beginning to have an effect on my body, which is building up again after losing weight on the trek. The vigorous exercise of the last month has given my muscles more tone and I feel very good.

The night's meal was salad, which I prepared. We have decided it is another successful formula we can use again. The vegetables used were so very cheap. It really is unbelievable: 10 paisa (less than a penny) for a lettuce, spring onions 50 paisa (4d), carrots 20 paisa (1½d).

'A large black bull nosed its way through the vegetable market'. To the left of the picture is the rare sight of another tourist.

Thursday 21st March

David ...

Much shopping, stocking up with the many essentials that are cheaper here than in India – rice, sugar, flour, coffee etc. John and I could hardly stagger back with our huge loads. Shopping was easier than the packing, which we left Johnny to do. Quite a surprise when 'The Camp' management invited us in for dinner tomorrow. So much for our planned early start; now we shall go as far as Daman with the hope of catching a last clear dawn to view the panorama before leaving.

When shopping early this morning I saw a man drop two bowls of yoghurt from his basket. Undismayed by the mess he was leaving, he went on. Dogs began to lick the scattered pot and yoghurt. A beggar fell in with them, scooping the milk up into the largest piece of the broken pot and drinking the dirty mess down. The dogs never moved; all drank as fast as they could to get a full share. Passers-by never gave a second glance at the fellow, down on his knees.

In the afternoon John and I spent an amazing half-hour in a local school. It was situated on the side of Durbar Square. Whenever we have passed the building it has sounded chaotic, like a playground during break. Today we ventured in and asked to be shown around.

Durbar Square.

It was a primary school with tiny classrooms crammed with children sitting at long desks. They were all were extremely noisy, coming and going as they pleased. Teachers did little except stand at the front. The walls were bare, the conditions cramped, the children restless: education, as we know it, just cannot function in the schools here.

Apart from the noise, I imagine the conditions are very similar to the Board Schools of the late 19th Century at home. All that the children can possibly get is from rote learning. Their textbooks give exercises that they follow in exact rotation to reach a set standard each year. Examinations test the standards before a child can move into a higher class. In each standard, children varied in age through about four years. Individual work in exercise books was purely repetition; two or three pages might contain one sentence, rewritten for no apparent reason, "I am a good boy." The pupils buy their own books; nothing is provided by the school save a little space to sit and work.

Several eccentric Europeans are in town just now, young people who have gone native. One girl is in full Sherpani outfit, a group of long-haired dirty youths in dhotis (thin cotton length wound round the legs, used by the lower Indian classes) and of combination outfits befitting the 'hi-travel' that these effect. (We noticed a type of person on our journey who very obviously wanted to appear experienced, carefree travellers. They would wear unusual or ethnic clothing. If they

Vegetables for sale in the streets of Kathmandu.

had vehicles, they would be splattered with mud. We called this phenomena 'high travel').

In the evening we went to the Everest restaurant for a luxury meal to celebrate our return to the West tomorrow. We had three Chinese dinners between five; amazing value and really excellently done. After savouring that, amid cries of "delicious", "marvellous", etc, we retired to the Camp Hotel for sweets and coffee.

So the half-way stage has come: we have done just over 9000 miles and spent just about half the money. Over a coffee we discussed plans for the return. The only essential is that we must arrive in Istanbul with £120 to £130 to allow us to cross Europe and reach home. With that sum in mind we can take as long as we like to get there.

I'm quite looking forward to being back on the road with our own organisation back in full swing.

❧

John ...

Dave and I went out in the morning to do the shopping for the return journey. We bought large quantities of sugar, flour, rice, porridge and corn flakes. I visited a Tibetan shop and saw some quite cheap, reasonable boots; I returned straight away with Pam and bought them for 23 rupees. I could have got them cheaper, I'm sure, but I wasn't quick-thinking enough.

After a light dinner Dave and I went off to look at a school; the Tourist Office had suggested the noisy one nearby. The headmaster was not there but a teacher offered to show us round. The classrooms were very small, with children absolutely crammed in. One side was open to the elements and in fact there were no doors, just two openings. Nothing seemed to be going on in any of the classrooms that we visited. The children were just sitting there with closed books in front of them. Apparently they had to buy their own textbooks and exercise books.

The classes were called 'standards' and it was necessary to pass an exam at the end of a year in order to go up into the next class. All the lessons seemed very repetitive and there was certainly little air of professionalism about the teachers. It seemed to me that this school was at least 50 years behind those in England. I should say it bore more resemblance to a 'dame school' than to Frecheville Junior School, my first teaching post.

We didn't stay long as the teacher didn't speak English very well. I bought a couple of textbooks from a nearby shop, which I would use on return to England. I returned to the Camp while Dave went off to do some more shopping.

That morning the management invited us to have dinner with them the next day. This meant we would start later than planned and spend the night at Daman.

I spent the latter part of the afternoon taking photographs of the city as I had very few so far. The light was good and I hoped they would come out well.

In the evening, about 6.00pm we went for our final celebratory nosh at the Everest. It was another fantastic Chinese meal, finished off with sweet and coffee at the Camp restaurant. It was early to bed that night because we had to be up early the next morning. It would be great to be back on the road.

Friday 22nd March

David ...

A very bright start with much to do before leaving this very pleasant city. A quick breakfast because we did not want to eat too much before our Nepali lunch. I did the remainder of the shopping while Johnny and the others packed our kit. Les went for 20 loaves to stock up. Slowly, things began to fit back into the Land Rover: still an amazing feat.

When all was packed and the others had returned from taking a few last-minute photographs, we went for lunch with the owners of the hotel. The management was ready for us and five glasses of water stood on the table. The 'father' of the team of management produced the rice, buffalo meat and vegetables, which were delicious and quickly eaten. We gathered that this must be the routine for guests who stay any length of time; a great gesture that makes one want to return.

After filling in the visitors' book and drinking one last milky tea in the Camp restaurant, we left to head west. Before leaving we had one last call at the post office to post 38 post cards and see if there was any mail.

Kathmandu fell behind as the road wound up towards Daman. Three road checks slowed us, as we had to fill in the usual forms. After four hours I was tired of the slow twisting road, often covered with debris from recent landslides. Teams of men and boys shovelled the mess over the edge to go rolling down the steep hillsides, continuing the scar from above the road.

The rich fields had grown good looking crops since we came through six weeks ago. Cereals, potatoes, beans and onions all look excellent. All the vegetables in Kathmandu this morning were superb. The Land Rover is not pulling well, but our rest to service it tomorrow should cure this.

The school in Basantapur Square, 'Tiny classrooms crammed with children sitting in long desks and whenever we passed the building it sounded chaotic, like a playground during break'.

After four hours of slowly climbing we topped the Daman ridge. Behind us, large cumulus clouds billowed on the peaks and far below a valley patched with green caught the last sun before it disappeared in a spectacle of red and gold. Les tried the tourist bungalow, but was amazed to be told it was 80 rupees per night. Even 'hot and cold' can't be worth that much. We could put up our own beds on the restaurant floor for five rupees each, but instead we have set up our small tents on the only flat patch for 200 miles, for free.

Almost satisfied by cheese salad, tangerine and custard, we are going to bed early to get up and see the dawn over the mountains – we hope.

A barefoot porter in Kathmandu. This was Kaman's usual work – at half of the pittance we paid him!

✄

Johnny woke me at 6.30am and I got up immediately. We had a light breakfast of cornflakes, peanut butter sandwiches and tea before setting to work on packing the Land Rover. I packed the roof-rack while Johnny packed the inside. Dave and Les did the shopping and Pam the washing up. Our tasks were almost completed by 9.00am, so Les and I went to take a few last-minute photos, mainly close-ups in my case. When I returned the others were waiting to have the meal with the management.

John ...

We were taken upstairs and invited to sit down in their living room. It was comfortable, if a little spartan. They served us rice, buffalo meat, vegetables and curried tomatoes. At the end we thanked them and signed the Visitors' Book; a very nice touch of hospitality that we all appreciated. Despite previous doubts about the place (before we got to Kathmandu that is) 'The Camp' had turned out to be an excellent place.

There were the final touches to make to our packing and then one last milky tea in the Camp Restaurant. As we were drinking, LP came in with a present for us – a stone-carving of Vishnu. Another nice gesture and I think we had all forgiven him and were sincere in our farewell wishes. After all, we'd all got drunk ourselves at times.

Left the city at midday. Two passport checks and a stop at the head of Kathmandu Valley to take photographs and prepare a quick lunch. There were fine views from there of the Kathmandu Valley, which was much more verdant than when we arrived. The green of the terraced fields and the rust-red of the hillside with steep and deep valleys made very pleasant scenery. We journeyed through this for some time before starting the long climb up the 30-mile hill to Daman. Up and up, round and round, it was tiring driving for several hours.

When we were eight miles from Daman we could see the place quite easily, only two or three miles away as the crow flies; the bends accounted for the other five miles. The houses near this road were being modernised, replacing thatched roofs with corrugated iron. This contrasted with the villages near the Chinese road out to Dolalghat and Tibet which remained unchanged. The Land Rover struggled a little and seemed to have lost some of its power.

At Daman we were unable to find any affordable accommodation. The restaurant people said we could sleep there for 5 rupees each, which was far too expensive, so we pitched the small tents at the side of the road. Ate a first rate salad in the Land Rover. From there we had good views of dark tree-covered hills and large cumulus clouds all but blocking out the distant peaks.

In the valley bottom the lime green and dark brown chequered pattern of the fields was lit up by the sun. Beautiful, airy and romantic;

Traditional carved eaves in central Kathmandu.

what a pity we hadn't camped on our trek. Gorgeous pinks at sunset. Dave and I were going to get up to watch dawn break over the beautiful array of peaks to be seen from here.

Saturday 23rd March

David ... Making sure we didn't disturb the others, John and I crept out at about 5.00am to view dawn and sunrise over the Himalaya. The moon, in its last quarter, was still high. Venus glittered brightly above the dark red band of daybreak. The mountains on the east of the chain were in stark black relief; those on the west were still hidden by darkness. Muffled by duvet jackets and carrying cameras we went to stand on the base of the viewing tower; the staircase was still locked. Annapurna II developed two large white ghostly faces that stood out from the pale grey-blue background.

As the light grew stronger, the blood-red turned to gold, the intermediate ridges turned from stark black to dark green. Makalu, Everest, Nuptse were distant bulks, easy to pick out, their silhouettes being as we expected. The tourist folder that supposedly names them all was only half right, giving Nuptse and Lhotse two separate peaks with Everest in between. We, who have been, know different! Even before, as readers, we could have been fairly sure, but now we can even make a fair guess at what the proper names should be.

Himachuli, Gauri Sankar, Ganesh Himal, Annapurna, Everest and every single lump of rock was perfectly clear from left to right, west to east. All slowly grew near and enormous, as below, the valley showed signs of life with the thatches billowing smoke. First to smile with the pink flush of day was Ganesh Himal. One triangle blushed, then faded as Himachuli took the spotlight. Its highest point and a ridge sweeping away from us held the sun for a long time, making the rest of its enormous bulk pale with envy. I snapped it.

The sun was climbing far behind the range where Everest lies. The mountains threw long straight shafts of shadow across the faintly mauve sky. Then it was with us, throwing a brilliant light on to the western range, hiding the eastern one with its strong glare. In its fresh warmth we had a delightful breakfast of cornflakes, boiled eggs and butter.

We had been joined at the viewing tower by a frail English youth who had arrived late last night. Knocking Johnny up had failed to gain him a berth in our packed Land Rover. This morning he made poor, sorrowful conversation about being cold since 3.00am. When people take on a task such as his, hitch-hiking to England, then they must accept the standards they set themselves. His equipment was so pathetic that he can expect to be cold in most places, let alone 8,000ft.

'Rose pink tipped the highest peaks and the day had begun'.

Johnny refused him a lift; we can't afford the weight, nor have we the space. I refused him breakfast; after all, we carefully plan to suit our finances and organisation; so should he. Rather mean attitude, but he knew what he was doing, just as we did.

We took a last long look before going over the ridge on a long descent that took three hours. We approached the river valley apprehensively, hoping that the road had been reopened. None of us fancied a deep fording. There was a barrier, but we nipped smartly round it. We had met several people in Kathmandu who had come up by road, so we were expecting the barrier. For about three miles there was nothing save a very poor surface; no blockages, no new slides. Perhaps 200 yards from the end, the new surface of chippings was just being rolled flat. Many hands waved us down but by turning down the bank it was possible to rejoin the track that swung back on to the road, completely missing the river. So all was well; our cheek had paid off.

Terraced fields near Daman.

Out of the herd of roller-followers stepped an oldish chap who waved his arms and yelled angrily at us. His face twisted in frustration. We all put our faces to the window and smiled like friendly tourists; he went 'white' and bared his teeth. I am sure I have never seen anyone quite so angry.

We camped at the Forest Rest House, our full rig up for the first time since Agra, two months ago. In the hot sun we started our many chores of washing and reorganising the Land Rover before finally going home. Two students who said they were from the Forestry Institute came for a chat, promising to come tomorrow to show us around the College, take us swimming and to play volley-ball. First we must do all the Land Rover jobs.

An astounding fact from John: Lahore was the halfway stage on our journey so far. It quite surprised us all.

John ...   Dave woke me at 5.00am. I got up quickly, not wishing to miss any of the dawn as the sky was crystal clear. As we walked along to the viewing tower the eastern sky was already silhouetting the peaks of the Everest range. In the west the faint ghost-like grey shape of Himachuli loomed out of the darkness. The viewing tower was locked,

156

so we just stood and gazed at the view. The sky slowly came to light with blue lines cut through the beige shadows of the peaks. Faint whites became brighter and the darkness turned to grey. Rose pink tipped the highest peaks and horizon and the day had begun.

While we were observing this beautiful, natural daily phenomenon, an English bloke joined us. He wore a bush hat and hobnailed boots, a hitchhiker with that usual hitchhiker's complexion. He was soon on the cadging line for lifts and breakfast. Last night he had seen Johnny and hinted about sleeping in the Land Rover. I wouldn't have minded these blokes, but I wished they would accept the conditions they set for themselves, instead of making you feel rotten because of more careful forward planning. We had also found in the past that they didn't want to know you if you had nothing to offer.

Breakfast by the roadside and then we left this pleasant little campsite and drove the last mile or so to the top of the pass. We stopped to take our last photographs of the Himalaya, it was a sad moment. More beautiful than ever, the mountains hung over a blue haze of foothills, framed by tall rhododendron trees.

Down the other side the going was monotonous, an endless succession of bends, often at alarming hairpin angles. We ignored the road block at the bottom and drove straight on (we weren't going through the fords again if we could help it). Everything went well, with no blockages or road swept away, but at the end we met the angriest person I have ever seen. We all adopted sickly grins and gave him happy waves, thus causing his face to take on even angrier proportions. He made us back away and take a 50-yard detour, but it was better than the fords.

After this it took us only ten minutes to reach Hetauda, where we went straight to the Forest Rest House. While the others waited to make the arrangements for camping, Dave and I walked into the village for oddments of food. Milk was more expensive than in Kathmandu, but tomatoes and bananas much cheaper (20 bananas for a shilling and 3-4lb of tomatoes for 8d).

When we returned, the tents were up and after a filling dinner, I set to work on my washing; a long job but one that needed doing. I finished towards sunset and was now ready for the morrow's work on the Land Rover. Two Nepalese teachers from the nearby college wandered up for a chat. They gave us more interesting information and invited us to look round the place the next day, play volley ball, and told us of a good spot to swim. They also ordered milk for us for the morning. They said that 'Tiger Tops' (a lodge in the Chitwan National Park) was near and worth a visit, but we had only one day left on our visa and so we couldn't go. They also recommended Corbett National Park in India, a must for the next week.

Sunday 24ᵗʰ March

David …   A good early start to our busy day, out and about at 6.00am in the clear blue morning. The sun lost no time in gaining power; just pottering about in it all day will really give us a tan, we hope.

We gave the Land Rover a thorough going over. Les did the 9,000 mile service; I scrubbed out the interior; John washed and waxed the exterior; then 'Johnny the Packer' took over. He repacked it to gain even more space. Where it all goes I don't know; maybe some bits deflate or something. We did very little else, other than a little run up the village for shopping. Quite a restful day before our journey out on to the Indian plains tomorrow. Raxaul will be the sudden re-introduction to the teeming masses in the streets.

❧

John …   Rose early again and cleared out the back of the Land Rover before breakfast. A beautiful day and it was clearly going to be hot.

After breakfast I washed and wax-polished the outside of the vehicle while Dave purged the interior and Les the engine. The day grew hotter and the Land Rover more beautiful. We had a morning tea break and worked on. Our friends of the previous night didn't turn up to show us round the college, nor did they follow up on their other invitations, which was a pity. The day was spent entirely on work with no play.

A good dinner break (these were getting much better and bigger as our appetites grew). Went to do a little shopping with Dave and Les in the Land Rover to give it a road test. An Indian tried to overcharge us for eggs, but we managed to beat him down. It served as a reminder

Clouds develop over the highest peaks as we leave Daman.

that soon we would be back in India and with it would come all the haggling and bartering to get fair prices.

Spent the afternoon helping Les and doing other odd maintenance jobs around the camp. We were now actually on the point of return, doing all the jobs we had done at Higham, but this time for the return. (Higham is a village just north of Barnsley. Dave's parents lived at Royd Hill Farm in the village and it proved to be an excellent base for us to prepare for our journey. There was plenty of space to spread out but more importantly some very supportive, long suffering parents who tolerated our coming and going. There were also beds and superb farmhouse breakfasts!). However, I felt only slight regret at heading for home. It had been a gradual turn-round with no definite point where we could feel nostalgic. I thought I would enjoy the trip home and though it wouldn't be as exciting and adventurous, I wouldn't have to worry about not accomplishing what we had set out to do (in fact it proved to be equally exciting and adventurous).

Another grand evening meal, but we found out it was the bananas and not the baking powder in the flour that tasted peculiar in our banana fritters and custard. The custard powder and peanut butter we bought in Kathmandu were proving to be very useful. We went to bed early and were completely ready for the morrow.

Monday 25th March

David …

I'm sitting in a rest house at Muzaffarpur. The air is balmy and the cooling fans are whirring overhead. Outside a cricket is chirping as a lizard scurries across the lounge ceiling. After such a long day, these conditions are wonderful.

We rose at 6.00am to begin our homeward trip. One of my superb breakfasts with toast instead of fried bread; I couldn't face that mustard oil again, neither the taste nor the smell.

By the time we were ready to leave, the sun was gaining power, a harbinger of the sultry plains of India. As we went south the roads grew steadily busier. Just one bullock cart, then a whole convoy, then a whole road full of them. People reappeared to fill in the gaps on the road side. Villages of small thatched houses made of rough branches filled in with mud, looked very shoddy. Quite how they withstand the monsoon I don't know.

Many patches of corn were being harvested. Men and women squatted in teams, cutting handfuls of corn with small sickles. Men collected the large bundles and filled the bullock carts. I can't imagine how they consider the bullock cart to be economical, because they carry such small loads. But there is no alternative. They could modify the carts by extending the sides.

Teams of men and oxen threshed a dirty dried crop, which I later examined to find it was a mixture of peas and another seed pod. Les suggested that one of them is an inferior crop of linseed. Teams of oxen and cattle walk round and round a central pole treading on the bed of the crop. Occasionally one of the men would throw the straw over and add a new supply. When all is done, women remove the straw and sweep up the seeds and dust into baskets. Later they will toss the seeds into the breeze to let the dust blow away. A man appeared who spoke reasonable English; he was some sort of agricultural adviser. From him we gathered that the main problem was irrigation and the lack of it.

Getting out of Nepal was no problem but getting into India was slow, very slow. At the police check-post we could not find any life, so we visited the Customs office first. After producing the carnet, which the superintendent read from end to end, we realised that it had not been valid for Nepal. Slowly he filled in his various books and then

The Forest Rest House in Hetauda our last stop in Nepal, where we prepared for our return to England.

our passports, chortling because we had not noticed that the Nepalese stamp was wrongly dated.

By the time we got back to the police check-post two men had arrived. One filled in the stamps, the other checked. Just as on our last visit the ink pad was dry and so saliva was applied liberally to the stamp pad to raise enough ink to mark the passports. He too dated all our passports for yesterday.

Outside in the turmoil a bullock cart reversed clumsily into the back of the Land Rover. John was furious and almost tipped both cart and animal down the bank!

John and I swept into town, confident with our knowledge from the previous visit. We shopped quickly and easily. Lunch was excellent, beneath a tree for shade. Only a small crowd gathered.

Half an hour later we ran out of petrol, about 12 miles from Motihari. Johnny took the jerry can and waved down a passing bus. We all lazed around in the sun, watching the threshing process. One and a half hours later Johnny returned, riding in a jeep armed to the teeth with policemen. Apparently it was taking money out to an agricultural project.

With a full tank, we headed for Muzaffarpur. One startling incident occurred when a lorry pulled out in front of us, nearly causing a disaster. John leapt out to give the grinning driver an angry verbal lashing. He took no notice but was good for our digestive systems!

161

About 7.00pm and tired from our first brush with the busy conditions, we washed and soothed in the first rest house. John cooked up a superb curry, plus banana fritters and custard that I added to the menu. Our meals really are superb these days. Everyone takes such pride in producing tasty, filling dishes.

❧

John ... We were packed and ready by 8.20am. It was a good start and we left the pleasant little rest house and journeyed on through the forested hills. However, we were soon out of them and down on the flat plains surging towards India. The mountains faded into the background and although we were still in Nepal, the culture was already Indian, with bullock carts and dhotis in profusion.

The Nepalese Customs formalities were quick and simple, but we found that our carnet had not been valid for Nepal. The Indian Customs were less quick and took ages with our papers, discovering that the Nepalese had stamped the previous day's date. Confusion reigned over in the Police Post and they also put the wrong date. One could develop no respect for their officials; they were scruffy and their offices were filthy. You begin to accept it and are quite surprised when you think back to Dover, Europe, or even Turkey come to that!

Dave and I shopped again. We knew Raxaul and had less trouble than before, although it still took us three quarters of an hour. Prices were reasonable, tomatoes particularly being very cheap, 9d for 4lb. We decided we must eat plenty of those. Shortly beyond Raxaul we stopped beneath the shade of trees and the usual crowd gathered — we knew that we were back in India, but it was good.

Twenty miles further on we ran out of petrol. Johnny leapt on a bus, which we had just overtaken, to go the last eight miles into Motihari. Whilst waiting for his return I spent the time writing this, sunbathing and entertaining the inevitable crowd. I wouldn't have minded the experience of travelling on that bus, packed to capacity, but it was better for only one to go for the sake of expense.

We had pushed the petrol tank several times and it had to happen sometime. I hoped we had learned a lesson from it. With a full tank we drove on to Muzaffarpur.

❧

As I was getting the petrol can down from the Land Rover, a bus came along the road. We flagged it down and in a second I was on board and rattling off towards town.

The bus journey was quite an experience with masses of people crammed inside. Even the driver had four people at the front with him. There seemed to be three conductors as it was impossible to move up and down the bus. However, after a rather hair-raising and noisy ride we reached Motihara. They refused to accept payment for the journey and took me to where I could get petrol. With many thanks I left them and set off for the main road, carrying ten litres of petrol, hoping to find a bus.

It was about a mile to the junction and I was somewhat hot by the time I got there. It was approximately 3.30pm and I found the bus to Raxaul wasn't due to arrive until 5.00pm. I decided to walk and had covered a mile without seeing another vehicle. However, just as the heat was becoming too much, a Jeep and trailer, full of police, pulled up for me. They managed to get me in and I found that they were carrying the payroll to a government farming centre. It did not seem to worry them that they had picked up a complete stranger. We were soon back at the Land Rover and with relief I put the petrol in the tank.

৯৮

We ate our fine evening meal on the veranda of the rest house as the sky drained from deep red to darkness. We thought how great it was to be on the road again. It was how we had imagined this trip, crickets chirping and mosquitoes and moths flooding towards the light. The day was very hot, too hot, but we had to get used to it now. All sorts of strange bird noises echoed through the large-leafed trees and, as I sat under the shade of the awning, I thought about how long we five had been together without seeing another human being we knew. For four and a half months now we had been living like this; it no longer seems like a long holiday, more like a way of life. Early parts of our journey seem like the dim and distant past. Lots of things that have happened are now forgotten and lost forever. I am thankful to have kept a log to record the bare essentials and to have a geographical mind to remember the route and scenery.

৯৮

John ...　Our journey continued through northern India, Pakistan and then via the Khyber Pass into Afghanistan. From there we travelled on through Iran, Turkey and Europe finally making our return to Barnsley just over three months later

Postscript

"Live life to the full, blend dream with the deed."
Geoffrey Winthrop Young

Of course as a child I had dreams. With a father who took us onto the hills of my mother's homeland in Wales to play 'Scott of the Antarctic' and 'Mallory and Irvine', how could I not have had dreams? Frank Smythe's books fed those dreams in my teenage years, but at the same time I feared that I lacked the money, the connections and, probably, the talent to take part in the great adventures of our era.

Winthrop Young's words haunted me. They represented a pathway to adventure. I realised that if our aims were modest and compatible with the funding that we must ourselves provide, we could indeed 'blend our dreams with the deed'. But perhaps more than anything, finding companions who were prepared to take on the challenges that even a modest journey like ours involved was a stroke of luck in life for which I shall always be grateful. That those companions were people that I both like and admire produced an experience that has sustained me throughout my life and that I look back on with enormous pleasure and satisfaction.

Reprising the experience through the process of bringing together our diaries, letters, maps, photographs and our memories, has been equally rewarding.

John

Letters Home

Before The Trek

David: Letter dated 17th February 1968, sent to my parents from Kathmandu

Dear All,

What a fantastic day. I must tell you all this before I can tell you of the last few days.

This morning we got ourselves a Sherpa; 'LP' is his name, a small, brown, happy guy. He is going to take us out to the base camp of Everest. We have had our visa extended for another month; yet another stamp in our passports. We also had to get a trekking permit to allow us to visit the prohibited area around Everest because it is within 25 miles of the Tibetan-Chinese border. LP speaks good English – well, sufficient English. He has been on several expeditions: twice he has been high on Everest and on several other famous peaks – Gauri Sankar, Cho Oyu and Nanga Parbat.

First thing he did was survey our equipment to decide what we needed to take with us. Then we went shopping for our supplies: rice, flour, sugar, candles etc. There is very little for sale between here and Namche Bazaar, which is 150 miles away – eggs and vegetables maybe. Yes 150 miles away: we will trek 150 miles out and then 150 miles back – from Barnsley to London and back again. LP looked after us in the market, even sending one lot of rice back and giving the shopkeeper a flea in his ear. We bought 15 lb of rice, 15 lb of sugar and 15 lb of flour. We don't have to take tents because he will arrange accommodation in the villages. LP will do all the cooking on wood fires. It all sounds fantastic. We leave on Monday the 19th at 7 o'clock in the morning, on the bus for the first 30 miles, and then we are off walking!

Since my last letter we left Benares to head for Kathmandu. The only thing to stop us was the mighty River Ganges. There are a few bridges but a ferry at Patna would be more convenient and save about 150 miles on the very crowded roads. The day we left Benares we reached Arrah. Just outside the town we had our first accident; we ran over a pig. We couldn't help it. It just dashed out into the road. A large crowd swept round us and we sat rather shocked. One man took control and waved us on. We reacted to his urgent hand waving by leaving rapidly. We thought that was the safest option.

At Patna we eventually found the ferry port. After much traipsing from office to office we found that the boat was on the other bank of the river. No one knew when it would be back but certainly not before the next day. We calculated the finance of it all and it proved to be considerably cheaper to use petrol than cross on the ferry so we motored round to the bridge. That stretch of road from Patna towards Calcutta was one long and huge crowd. I have never seen so many people. Every inch was like Barnsley market at its very busiest: every inch, every single street. Once out of the towns the villages are all straw and reed dwellings set among bamboo and banana groves. I have had fresh bananas straight from the tree. The surrounding fields are rich cereal and rice crops. So much of the fertile land is devoted to growing spices. All one day we passed nothing but red pepper fields. There were vast areas, like red sea shores, where the peppers had been put out in the sun to dry. No matter how hard we looked north we could never see the Himalaya.

Crossing the border was the usual laugh. We shot past everything into Nepal, then had to reverse back into India. Only six sets of identical forms at the three offices, each one more dilapidated than the last. The officer had to spit onto the ink pad to be able to stamp our passports. The police post was left vacant so we just filled the forms in ourselves and then left. A man arrived with a bag that contained a mongoose and a snake. He wanted us to pay him to see them fight. The border was a very narrow bridge over a railway line. As we sat among the constant stream of bullock carts, tongas and trishaws a bullock cart lost its wheel and blocked the whole road for about an hour. No one bothers; they just sit around spitting. Every man, woman and child spits, deep-throated spits. When walking around we have to dance to avoid the constant battery of spitting.

As soon as we crossed the border the culture changed. There were still many Indians about but the small Nepalese men in their cotton, plant pot hats look much fitter.

Once clear of the border town all forms of transport disappeared. Nepalese peasants carry everything in enormous packs suspended on a band over their foreheads. Sherpa porters carry 80-100 lb with ease, all day, uphill and down dale. Next day we began the climb to Kathmandu. The road is well known for landslide blockages. Sure enough, after ten miles, when we were still on the flat, the road was blocked. We had to turn into the river bed to avoid the landslide.

The first ford was no trouble, though the water was deep and rushing. The second and third wet the plugs a bit but they dried out quickly. The fourth stopped us mid-stream and we all jumped out up to our knees in water. Fortunately Les got the engine to fire, only on two cylinders, but enough to prevent the water getting up the exhaust. Slowly in four-wheel drive 14 SRB crawled out none the worse for our panic. At the top of the hill some three hours later Les found we had broken a back spring. We have had our spare fitted for the equivalent of 13/6d.

Altogether we climbed for four hours before reaching the top of the pass. All the hillsides are terraced wherever possible. Vegetables and rice are grown on these small terraced fields. People live in small houses scattered across the hillsides and valleys. From the top we could see all we came for – 300 miles of mountains from Annapurna on the left to Everest on the right – the mighty Himalaya. John was beside himself with excitement.

Next day we established ourselves in the Camp Hotel, a hotel for travellers. There are similar places in most towns and we usually hear about them from other travellers. This one is cheap and satisfactory for our needs.

Next we arranged to go and see the Princess. Out came my super white shirt and carefully preserved white handkerchief and I had my shoes cleaned by a boy in the street. We all looked very smart. We were picked up in the car of the Kumar, her husband, at a travel agent's who had arranged the visit and thought it unwise to be picked up at the

Camp. In their bungalow we chatted for about one and a half hours. Les shot one cake all over the carpet. Johnny very nearly spilled his tea on the settee. Les left his lighter and had to collect it the next day. As we left after a very pleasant time the Kumar offered to solve our problem. We had nowhere to leave the Land Rover while we went trekking so he is going to move a few carriages for us to put 14 SRB into the royal garages for a month.

Kathmandu and the surrounding villages are straight out of the Middle Ages – narrow streets, timbered houses, low overhanging eaves, open sewers/drains, stand pipes and wells. It was all exactly as I imagine life would have been in England in the 15th and 16th Centuries. Nepalese farmers carry their loads of vegetables into the city on yokes over their shoulders or in huge packs on their backs. There are four- or five- storey pagodas everywhere. There is no glass in any of the windows. A wooden grille, often beautifully carved, covers the window space to give some privacy.

Life in the streets is fantastic. People squat with their vegetable produce for sale at very cheap prices. Small shops sell absolutely everything: Farex Rusks, chocolate, Horlicks, Gillette from the West, through to local prayer wheels and cheap plastic from the Far East.

I collected lots of mail today. I will write to everyone when I return from the mountains. We should be away for a month so you will not hear from me in that time.

We can thank Mrs Robinson (a close friend of my mother who helped in many ways, particularly with her sewing machine) for her perfect mosquito nets. We have used them a lot in India. We finished off her lovely cake to celebrate our arrival in Kathmandu and just over 9000 miles of driving. We now bless Mrs Smith for her one million plastic bags which we shall use to pack all the foodstuffs for the trek, plus the lightweight bowls to eat from

There are many Tibetans around with their really fabulous faces, topknots of long hair, long black cloaks-cum-overcoats and high woven boots. They are all trying to sell 'genuine' Tibetan relics of the Dalai Llama.

We shall leave Kathmandu for Delhi about the 24th March.

John: Letter dated 17ᵗʰ February 1968, sent to my parents from Kathmandu

14ᵗʰ February

After we left Benares we headed straight for Kathmandu. The journey took four days and we are all glad to be out of India and into the mountains of Nepal. My letters will probably have created a very bad impression of India. It is squalid but the countryside has very much to be said for it. It is a mystic land and the moonlit nights are quite marvellous. Nevertheless we drove from Benares with a desire to speed away from the crowded plains. As we moved down the Ganges the weather became very hot and the nights were uncomfortably humid, with mosquito nets essential and a strong chorus of crickets outside. Around the Patna area the crowds were even thicker and the city itself stretched for ten miles – just one long teeming throng which you had to blast your way through (with the horn) at about ten miles an hour.

At the Nepal border we still couldn't see the mountains but nevertheless the invisible barrier the border creates had effected a big change in culture and people's appearance. Then the mountains appeared as a thin line breaking out of the hazy horizon. What a thrill after a day's eager anticipation, and all eyes fixed firmly on the horizon. They drew closer and soon we were winding up forested hills, which were a great relief after over a month on flat plains. We spent that night in a beautiful little rest house just before the real foothills start.

Next day as we started to climb the road had a barrier across and a diversion was signposted. A track led onto the river bed until, we came to a ford; it was deeper than we expected but we got through all right. However we came to another which looked terribly deep. We plunged through and half-way across the unthinkable happened – the engine stalled. A look of panic crossed Les's face as he tried, to re-start the engine and Dave and I leapt out into thigh-deep water and. waded round to the back. Fortunately the exhaust pipe was an inch above the water. The starter motor rattled and eventually to our relief the engine spluttered back into life. Spurts of water poured out of the exhaust and all was well with, the engine. However, if it was to have enough power to break the water-resistance it had to be in 4-wheel drive and I had to feel under water for the relevant nut to turn with the wheel brace. With that done the Land Rover pulled out easily. A nasty few moments but we escaped with nothing worse than four wet pairs of trousers.

The next part of the road just bent and wound upwards through terraced hillsides for 8,000ft. It made Swiss passes look like Mottleash Hill. At the top we gained our first glimpse of the 'eternal snows' as an immense snow peak peeped through the trees. Then we gained a fantastic view of an inconceivably large array of peaks and snowfields. We could see Kanchenjunga, Everest, Gauri Sanker, The Fishes Tail, Annapurna and Dhaulagiri – all the world's greatest peaks around which are wrapped the greatest and most thrilling mountain adventure stories. Vast and indescribably beautiful they almost brought tears to my eyes. I wished you all could see it – no wonder they worship the mountains. The Everest group (it was difficult to pick out the actual summit) was the most impressive jumbled mass of fluted ice walls and towering peaks. It was an irresistible challenge to go amongst them and I hope we can satisfy our urge.

When we reached Kathmandu we were unable to find a campsite and are staying at a cheap hotel (13/- night for all of us). It is dirty outside, but quite clean and quaint inside. It used to be the well-known hangout of beatniks and hippies, but they've all been kicked out.

Today we have been enquiring about walking to the foot of Mount Everest. It is 150 miles away (300 miles return) but everyone, including Les and Pam are keen to go. We should get the permission for which we applied today and we have provisionally booked a Sherpa Porter (for 10 Rps a day, about 6/8d). There are a few maps of the area and so it is quite important to have one from the point of view of route finding. White shirts are washed and shoes cleaned in readiness for tomorrow when we shall be picked up by car to go and visit the Princess.

Robert asked about language difficulties. Well of course sign language works with everyone. Nevertheless ever since Turkey, i.e. Iran, Pakistan, India and Nepal, we have never had trouble in finding someone who speaks English. In fact in parts of India, Pakistan and Nepal there are more signs in English than in their native tongue. In Nepal surprisingly I would estimate that almost 25% of the entire population speak English. Language has hardly been a problem at all.

15th February

Well we have just returned from the Royal bungalow after spending two hours there and having tea and cakes. We waited at the rendezvous at 4.00pm and were picked up by the chauffeur in the royal Volkswagon. At the gate of the bungalow a flunkey rushed to open the door and let us in. Another flunkey opened the car door and we were led into a beautiful sitting room with two fabulous white dogs. (They were wonderful, especially compared with the skeleton dogs we saw in India.) The Kumar (Prince) made his entry and from then on things were pretty informal. We chatted about Nepal and Britain and were served with tea and cakes. Then the Princess made her entrance but she is either shy or doesn't speak English, so we didn't have any conversation with her. He showed us the album of their visit to England, which the Queen had presented to them, and in it we saw photos of O.B.M.S.(U) with Lester Davies and Allan Roberts.

We have been having trouble finding somewhere to leave the Land Rover whilst we are walking to Everest. We broached the problem and the Kumar said we could leave it at one of their garages at the new 'palace' they are having built. An excellent two hours and we achieved one of our major objectives. Les, of course, scattered cake crumbs over the palace floor and caused an incident by leaving his cigarette lighter in the palace. We were driven back again by the chauffeur.

That seems to be most of the news to date – the log is still going well (about two pages per day) – so you can read in closer detail when we get back. Things are pretty backward around Base Camp on Mount Everest. 30 days is the standard time; I am hoping to cut down on that. It should be lovely in the 'high hills' with a Sherpa to cook our meals and to sit round a wood fire under the stars. We have received official permission today to go right up to base camp on the Khumbu Glacier. I hope we manage it, it has been my ambition for some time. We hope to be in Kathmandu for six weeks unless you hear to the contrary.

Love John

❧

Les: Letter dated 16th February 1968, sent to my family from Kathmandu

Dear Mum and Dad, Baz and Hil, Caroline, Jane and Helen,

We are now in Kathmandu after an eventful journey from Benares. On leaving Benares we went to Patna which was an awful place, filthy and overcrowded. We were going to cross the Ganges there but the ferry was on the other side of the river at the time and as usual we couldn't get any sense out of the officials so we had to go about 50 miles downriver to cross at the nearest bridge. From there we went north through Muzaffarpur to the Nepalese border. On the way I ran over a pig which shot out in front of the Land-Rover.

Our first night in Nepal was spent just inside the border at a small rest house in the foothills. It was a refreshing change not to be surrounded by people and to see hills again after being in the hot and densely populated Ganges valley. The following morning we set off for Kathmandu. The road climbed higher and higher up the valley and in most parts was quite good. At one point however it was being repaired and the diversion took us along the valley bottom causing us to cross the river several times by means of some fairly deep fords. Several times the engine misfired because of water on the distributor and eventually, in the middle of the deepest ford, it stopped completely. Fortunately the exhaust pipe was about an inch above the water so it didn't flood the engine. If it had we would have been in trouble. As it was, all the others got their feet and trousers wet when they got out to push (I was driving). The engine started again eventually and I managed to drive out.

The rest of the journey was uneventful along the most beautiful road we have come across. The scenery is magnificent, very hilly with terraced fields all along the valleys, planted with rice. That morning we also got our first view of the high Himalaya – Everest, Annapurna, Kanchenjunga etcetera, covered with snow and looking as though they were floating in the sky, all of a hundred miles away.

We arrived in Kathmandu late that afternoon and had to set ourselves up in a cheap hotel because there is nowhere to camp here. Actually it's not too bad and full of people similar to us, apart from a few hippies, and in fact there is a line of Land Rovers parked outside. There has been a continual stream of Nepalese here trying to buy them for ridiculous prices. We have had $1000 offered for ours.

As soon as we arrived in Kathmandu John got in contact with the Prince, with the result that we went round for tea yesterday afternoon. They don't live in the palace but in a fairly ordinary bungalow – although that is only a temporary residence. We didn't discover whether the Princess spoke English or not because she didn't say a word, but he was a very pleasant chap.

We are going trekking to the foot of Everest in a few days and we have had trouble finding a safe place to leave the Land Rover. When we mentioned this to the Prince he said they had a garage which he would clear for us in their new palace, which is being prepared for them. He said there were a few carriages in it at the moment.

We are now awaiting the return of a Sherpa with another trekking party so that he can come with us as a guide and porter on the trek. It is about a 300-mile round trip, all on foot, and should take about a month.

17th February

The Sherpa arrived today so we have been busy getting in supplies of rice, sugar, porridge etc. He is carrying most of our stuff and is going to do the cooking all for 10 rupees a day (about 7s.). He seems quite a good fellow and has been up to the South Col of Everest with an American expedition. We are setting off the day after tomorrow and won't be back until about the 20th of March and we have to leave Kathmandu on the 24th. I will write again when we get back to Kathmandu to tell you of our anticipated movements from then on.

Love Les

৯

Letters Home After The Trek

David: Letter dated 18th March 1968, sent to my parents from Kathmandu

Dear All,

We are safely back after a fantastic 28 days out of civilisation: no roads, not even a wheel, no progress visible at all. It was quite amazing that we could journey outward for 15 days and leave behind all we regard as civilisation; the only bits of the 20th Century have been left behind by expeditions – vacuum flasks, airbeds, a variety of tins and oddments of clothing. Otherwise life cannot have changed much for centuries.

Corn is ground by pounding in a bowl or between hand-powered grindstones. Rice is polished by using a foot-powered plunger that strips off the husks. In a few places water is used to turn small grindstones that turn the cereals into flour. All agriculture is done on terraces cut into the hillsides. Wherever it is possible the steps cut out to make the terraces begin right in the valley bottom. Houses of the larger families either sit amid their 'estate' or squat in small groups of maybe half a dozen near water. Animals – goats, cattle and chickens – live on the ground floor, with the family upstairs.

The houses of the Nepalese differ from those of the Sherpas; in fact the whole culture differs. Sherpas are far more connected to the Tibetans, racially and as Buddhists. Nepalese are Hindus. Nepalese houses are thatched with a few tiny windows upstairs. They have few possessions other than water containers and eating utensils, dishes, cups and ladles. Sherpa houses have slates made from split timber held down by rocks. The walls are far more substantial but have the same tiny windows covered by shutters. There is no glass in either kind of house. Inside it is very dark. Thank goodness they are all the same pattern or we would never have found our way about.

During the first few days we slept on the leaky verandas of the Nepalese houses. We have gathered fleas in our sleeping bags, manure on the outsides from the animals traipsing in and out. Goats and cattle spend the day tethered about a yard from the door. At night they are brought inside the house. All the fodder is brought by the women or children from the woods where the land is too steep to build terraces.

Thank goodness for Mrs Smith's polybags, which we used as groundsheets when it was dry or as covers for our sleeping bags when it rained in on the verandas. As we got into the higher areas we slept inside the Sherpa houses, on the floor along with everyone else. Sherpas are such a friendly, happy and hospitable people. Of course standards are so very different from ours. Children just mess anywhere on the floor, amid the mess of their other daily doo-doos. Chickens wander in and add their lucky piles.

None of the houses has a chimney so smoke fills the house and then escapes where ever it can, through holes in the roof, walls or doorways and windows. Consequently the faces of people are black from always sitting around wood fires. The whole of the inside of the roof and walls are black and shiny with tar. Soot-webs cover the roof.

Beds are usually near the fire for mum and dad and as many of the young under-eights that can get in. They consist of dried leaves covered in rags and maybe a sheepskin. Other members of the family have a blanket and settle down with any lodgers that have called in for the night. All people on the move just stay in the most convenient house as dusk falls. One night we were in a house that had 21 visitors, including us. We all fitted neatly into one room, plus the family of eight. I slept alongside three female porters, Sherpanis.

Everything that needs transporting in Nepal, in Kathmandu and then out into the countryside, is carried by porters. Porters usually get a rupee per day for every ten kilos they carry. Usually they carry about 100lb in their baskets slung on their headbands. Our porter carried about 90lb with ease, all day up and down and I think I weigh about a stone more than him.

We passed lines of porters carrying absolutely everything, including long zinc pipes for a water supply that is being paid for by the New Zealand Sherpa Trust Fund. It is quite common for a village or house to be up to half an hour from water – either up or down hill. Nepalese use large brass vases carried on the hip to collect their water, about four gallons at a time. Sherpas have a large oval staved cask slung on their headband that must hold at least ten gallons. They tip the water into large copper bowls. No one grumbles when they find that the water supply is low; they just go and collect fresh supplies.

We all slogged uphill and down deep valleys, only to have to climb up the other side again. It was damned hard work. We sweated a lot but eventually got really fit so that though everyday was tiring we got over the stiff muscles. Johnny suffered from terrible blisters. We all lost weight because we were using up all our energy every day for 27 days. We ate well and our appetites grew to such proportions that we could not be filled. We all grew pretty sick of rice and curry.

The tracks we had to follow were easy to see but always difficult to walk on; they are steep, loose rocks and stones and rutted by water. I had to concentrate on every step so as to avoid a slip or a trip. When I got tired I found a trip a real waste of energy.

Seeing the mountains on the way out was amazing; such huge snow-covered bulks always filling the horizon. Each afternoon the clouds would build up and hide the peaks until a bright dawn revealed them again.

On a normal day we got up about 5.30 to 6.00am. We had porridge and tea and then walked for about three hours before stopping for dinner of rice and curry and tea. Another four hours of walking and then evening meal of rice and curry and cocoa. Then to bed by 7.30pm at the latest, and glad to be there.

After 12 days we were among the really high mountains. We reached Namche Bazaar on the thirteenth day. It is the largest village up there with about 50 houses. It is where expeditions usually gather their supplies together before heading out to Tengboche. In Namche we hired a high-altitude porter to take over from Kaman who would have suffered at the higher altitudes. Namche is at about 11,000ft. All around are huge and high peaks.

Next day we left for Base Camp. Along the valley we went to Tengboche Monastery where we had lunch. Giants stood all around us in the glorious weather. Everest peeped over Nuptse and Ama Dablam filled the sky. That night we slept in the poorest and dirtiest house of all at Pangboche at 14,000ft. Altitude began to tell and after two hours sleep I woke with a violent headache, which is normal as we acclimatise. Next day we moved up to Pheriche, which is a collection of hovels and yak pastures used in the summer. There was only one boy there looking after the yaks belonging to the monastery. I can't describe the peaks; by then they were so big and snow covered that we could hardly believe it.

As we began our last trek up towards the Base Camp it began to snow. For three hours we trudged up with great piles of firewood on our back. Our hearts sank to have travelled all that way to find such awful weather. That night we stayed at Lobuche which is about four miles from Base Camp, in an old yak house. Just an old dry stone building with a roof full of holes. I didn't manage much sleep there because we were at 16,000ft; whenever I moved in my head-ache-sleep I would wake up gasping for oxygen.

Dawn revealed a perfect day, no cloud, no haze, bright sun, and fresh snow gleamed on the faces of the mountains. Avalanches crunched down the gullies and faces on Nuptse. Two hours of puffing and panting brought us to Gorak Shep below the Khumbu Icefall that is such a difficult start for the climbers on Everest. No words of mine can tell you of the majesty of the scene; the enormous bulk of Everest, the peak of Pumori and the pass into Tibet.

From Gorak Shep we climbed Kala Pattar, which rises to 18,200ft and serves as a viewing tower for the ring of kings and queens of mountains. It was hard work getting up to that height; ten or 12 steps, rest, gasp, up, gasp, and so on. John and Johnny suffered from altitude sickness. Pam was exhausted. I was fittest on the day.

So we achieved our first goal, the top of the Kala Pattar.

From the top we took our first turn back to the west; a dramatic turning point for our expedition. We are now on our way home. That night was sleepless again though we were really exhausted. Next day we descended right down to Tengboche for a great night's sleep. Pam had to sleep in the only house for women in the monastic village.

Next day we left Namche for Kathmandu. We were so eager to be back we covered the distance in eight days. It took us 13 days going out.

The one thing that marred the expedition was our Sherpa. When we reached his own village and territory, nine days out, he got drunk. We forgave him because he hadn't been home for a year. When he made a habit of it and became a real drag on our progress over four days, we sacked him. Kaman, our porter, took over. By then we knew the ropes and enjoyed ourselves even more without him.

On the last uphill stretch I developed a sore tendon in my right ankle. Fortunately it only hurt on the uphill and by the time it became really painful we had only downhill to the road to come. We reached the road about 4.30pm to find there was no transport until 6.00am the next day. We spent another night on a veranda beneath a huge full moon.

Kathmandu almost seemed like home as we set about recovering. For two days now all I have done is rest, eat, rest my tendon, eat. Strange how the monotony of our diet made us dream of all our favourite foods: Black Magic, chocolate digestives, stew meat and gravy with chips, egg and beans, a pear, a Granny Smiths, a glass of milk. Tortuous to think about them but we had long conversations and planned our menus for Kathmandu. I have released the purse strings, a bit, to ensure a real treat for a few days.

From here we are going to Delhi and then Lahore.

Love David

John: Letter dated 17th March 1968, sent to my parents from Kathmandu

The Camp Hotel,

Dear Mum and Dad,

We have stood at the foot of Mount Everest and gazed up at its rocky ramparts. We climbed Mount Kala Pattar (18,200ft) at Everest's foot, mainly to get good views. The turning point of our whole expedition came when we turned to face westwards at Base Camp. The journey took 27 days during which time we were completely cut off from civilisation – we didn't even see a wheel, let alone a car. A real month in the Middle Ages. We spent the nights living in the homes of Nepalese and Sherpa hill people.

The outward journey to Namche Bazaar took 13 days – 120 miles over 9,000ft or 10,000ft ridges – up and down all the way, with hardly a flat stretch. The route varied from deep sub-tropical river valleys where gaily coloured birds chattered as they fluttered between gaudy flowers or into trees with enormous leaves, to high snow-covered mountain passes through sweet-smelling pine forests and beautiful rhododendron slopes.

Much of the early part of the journey was through terraced fields where rice and maize were growing. At these lower altitudes we stayed on the verandas; they were just too dirty and smoky inside. They don't use chimneys and so we were sleeping more or less in the open. Later on at higher altitudes we stayed actually inside Sherpa houses. The Sherpas are remarkably friendly and hospitable and you soon take to them.

All the way the scenery was marvellous with good views of some of the highest summits. On the 13th day as we plodded up the final path to Namche Bazaar we rounded a corner and there it was – Mount Everest – a solid rock giant peeping over the precipices of Nuptse.

At Namche we hired a high-altitude porter and continued past the monastery of Tengboche to spend the night at Pangboche. The next night we slept in a barn at an altitude of 16,000ft. The following day we made a dash for Base Camp and Mount Kala Pattar. We suffered tremendously from altitude and I can quite honestly say we have never pushed ourselves harder on a mountain.

On top it was worth it and we could see from close range all those read-about features of the 'Mother Goddess of the Snows'. Over to the left we could see China through the Lho La Pass, and many other peaks such as Ama Dablam. The immensity and staggeringly spectacular nature of these mountains are very conducive to the idea of their being 'gods'. It's like another world up there – I've seen the 'Kings of the Alps' but they're nothing compared with these. They stand before you and yet are so remote, untouchable and infinitely inaccessible. I admire the men who climb them and would give anything to have a go myself.

As we turned to return to the barn we realised that we had reached our furthest point east and from then on we would travel into the setting sun. In two days' time we were back in Namche and fully recovered for our return journey.

LP, our Sherpa, had been a grand little fellow on the way out, cooking for us in the evening and mid-day as we would flop exhausted on the floor, haggling for fair prices for firewood, rice and chickens that we bought, and he really looked after us. Kaman, our porter, has also done well throughout, carrying 80lb and washing up and lighting fires for us. He amazed us by walking barefoot – but absolutely staggered us when he walked barefoot in the snow for a day. What fantastic people they are.

Unfortunately LP had a reputation for getting drunk and the fourth time, after delaying us for three hours on the second day of our return, we had no alternative but to sack him. It left us in a bit of a spot and gave the trip a new air of excitement and adventure. Fortunately by this stage we knew the ropes and with Kaman, our faithful porter, we made the return journey in the very good time of eight days.

Kaman impressed us all, a poor but simple and honest man who stuck with us, and by sign language we came to know him very well. We paid LP 6s 8d per day as the skilled man and Kaman, as the porter, only 5s 4d per day. Kaman took over many of LP's duties and so on our return to Kathmandu we gave him 20 rupees (13s 8d) as a bonus - his eyes filled with delight. It would have been worth the expense at double the price

During the trip I was bitten mercilessly by fleas and I am covered in bites. We also began to get tired of our diet which consisted of a big bowl of porridge in the morning and rice and curry, or chapattis and curry for dinner and evening meal. At Namche Bazaar, Kathmandu seemed remote.. It was like a separate expedition – 27 days is a long time, and it felt longer than we had imagined when we set off. We sat there eating curry and dreaming of the pleasures that awaited in Kathmandu – fried eggs, I never thought I'd have such a craving for them.

Yesterday we hit town and since then have been celebrating with a high protein diet. Last night we ate in a restaurant and have had the most fantastic Chinese meal. Today, more eating and relaxing.

For me, this has been the best month of the whole trip and a wonderful insight into how these mountain people live. My brief log is wholly inadequate to describe what we have seen. We are now going to spend a few days in Kathmandu before driving back to Delhi where we should arrive within the next fortnight. From there we shall go to Kangra for as long as we can in order to do some climbing. From there back to Lahore and then to Rawalpindi, Peshawar, the Khyber Pass and Kabul and, probably late June or early July, back in England.

Love John

Before and After

A series of photographs taken in the same places over 40 years apart. They were taken on the return visit in 2010. Those around Namche Bazaar and Everest were taken by John's son Owen and his wife Julie on their honeymoon in 2010.

A barber's shop just off Durbar Square.

Hanuman Dhoka Road, Kathmandu in 1968 …

… and in 2010. Much has changed but the shops are still selling the same things.

183

Hanuman Dhoka Palace.

1968

2010

The road where
the Camp Hotel
used to be.

The very place where Les complained at having to walk '300 bloody miles'.

The village of Namde where we stayed both on the way out and the way back.

1968

2010

Namche Bazaar.

Near Pheriche looking South.

Looking towards the Khumbu Glacier from Pheriche.

188

1968

2010

Lobuche looking North.

Biographies

David Peckett

Born 1941 and brought up on his parent's farm just North of Barnsley. At the age of 11 he contracted tuberculosis of the right hip which led to three years in hospital and a permanent disability which severely curtailed participation in the sports he loved. He missed 3 years of schooling and started work at Samuel Fox's steelworks in Stocksbridge as an Industrial Chemist, after doing 'O' levels at the age of 18. In 1961 his interest in craft led to Sheffield Teacher Training College where he trained to teach English, woodwork and metalwork. In 2001 he retired as Senior Inspector for Primary Education in Wakefield.

John Driskell

Born 1943 and brought up in Scunthorpe, spending long holidays every year at his grandparents' home in South Wales. His interest in mountains became all consuming and in 1961 he chose Sheffield,to train to be a teacher as many climbers do because of easy access to the Peak District. He studied geography. In 1966 he became an instructor at Ullswater Outward Bound School. His love of mountains, climbing and travel has taken him all over the world. A brain haemorrhage in 1972 altered his life profoundly but not his enthusiasm. He retired in 2000 after 23 years as a head teacher in primary schools.

Les Simms

Born 1943 and brought up in Scunthorpe. With John he attended Scunthorpe Grammar School and despite a keen and lasting interest in art, craft and music he went on to obtain a degree in Pharmacy in Leicester. He took a PGCE at Sheffield Training College in 1966. He enjoyed some sports including cricket and badminton which he still plays, but certainly not those which required a real measure of physical effort. He retired in 2003 after over 30 years as a pharmacist in Pitlochry. (John and Les are cousins. Their grandmothers were identical twins and married to serving soldiers in the Third Dragoon Guards, who spent considerable time in India)

Johnny Rudd

Born 1943 and brought up in Wigton, Cumberland. A talented sportsman with a love of rugby and tennis he was a particularly good cross country runner who achieved top places in national competitions whilst at school. In 1961 he went to Sheffield Teacher Training College to study PE and Geography and went on to be a PE teacher in Manchester. He retired in 2002 after 20 years as a primary headteacher and now lives in France.

Pam Archer

Born 1942 and brought up in Blackburn. She trained as a teacher at Sheffield City Training College in 1961 where she studied Art and French, spending six months at a University in Tours. After qualifying she spent a year in a *lycée* on the outskirts of Paris and then taught in Sheffield. On returning from Nepal she settled in Manchester where she brought up three children. She has lost the urge to travel far and wide, but still loves walking in the English countryside.

Glossary

Chang: the rice or barley flour beer brewed by the locals in the villages.

Chorten: a wayside Buddhist shrine.

Col: dip in a ridge that makes it an easier route over the pass. The most famous is the South Col on Everest.

Cwm: Welsh name for a deep rounded valley set in the side of a hill or mountain

Graunch: (slang) long slow walk up a steep hillside that is very hard work.

Kangra: seen on photographs on the front of the Land Rover). We had intended to do some climbing in the Kangra area of Northern India, but permission to go there was refused, two weeks before we left England.

Kukri: a short curved knife used by the Nepalese.

Mani wall: a stone wall of slabs or boulders carved with prayers.

Rest house: rest houses, sometimes called *dak bungalows* were a network of houses built throughout the Indian sub-continent for the use of visiting government officials. In the 50s, 60s and perhaps for longer, Westerners were often allowed to stay in them. The prices ranged from totally free to very cheap.

Resting places: constructed of stone or wood alongside a path, beneath shade, for porters to rest their packs on.

Sherpa: an ethnic group, linked to Tibet and Buddhist history, that lives in the higher regions of Nepal.

Sherpani: a female Sherpa.

Sirdar: the head Sherpa on an expedition.

Stupa: a domed Buddhist shrine built near a village

Thrape: (slang) a long, hot, sweaty walk uphill that is hard work.